Cambridge Elements

Elements in Sociolinguistics
edited by
Rajend Mesthrie
University of Cape Town
Valerie Fridland
University of Nevada, Reno

LANGUAGE AND PLACE

Katie Carmichael
Virginia Tech

Paul E. Reed
University of Alabama

Shaftesbury Road, Cambridge CB2 8EA, United Kingdom

One Liberty Plaza, 20th Floor, New York, NY 10006, USA

477 Williamstown Road, Port Melbourne, VIC 3207, Australia

314–321, 3rd Floor, Plot 3, Splendor Forum, Jasola District Centre, New Delhi – 110025, India

103 Penang Road, #05-06/07, Visioncrest Commercial, Singapore 238467

Cambridge University Press is part of Cambridge University Press & Assessment, a department of the University of Cambridge.

We share the University's mission to contribute to society through the pursuit of education, learning and research at the highest international levels of excellence.

www.cambridge.org
Information on this title: www.cambridge.org/9781009517287
DOI: 10.1017/9781009380874

© Katie Carmichael and Paul E. Reed 2025

This publication is in copyright. Subject to statutory exception and to the provisions of relevant collective licensing agreements, with the exception of the Creative Commons version the link for which is provided below, no reproduction of any part may take place without the written permission of Cambridge University Press & Assessment.

An online version of this work is published at doi.org/10.1017/9781009380874 under a Creative Commons Open Access license CC-BY-NC 4.0 which permits re-use, distribution and reproduction in any medium for non-commercial purposes providing appropriate credit to the original work is given and any changes made are indicated. To view a copy of this license visit https://creativecommons.org/licenses/by-nc/4.0

When citing this work, please include a reference to the DOI 10.1017/9781009380874

First published 2025

A catalogue record for this publication is available from the British Library

ISBN 978-1-009-51728-7 Hardback
ISBN 978-1-009-38086-7 Paperback
ISSN 2754-5539 (online)
ISSN 2754-5520 (print)

Additional resources for this publication at www.cambridge.org/EISO_Carmichael

Cambridge University Press & Assessment has no responsibility for the persistence or accuracy of URLs for external or third-party internet websites referred to in this publication and does not guarantee that any content on such websites is, or will remain, accurate or appropriate.

Language and Place

Elements in Sociolinguistics

DOI: 10.1017/9781009380874
First published online: January 2025

Katie Carmichael
Virginia Tech

Paul E. Reed
University of Alabama

Author for correspondence: Katie Carmichael, katcarm@vt.edu

Abstract: Place has been central to sociolinguistic research from the very earliest studies. How speakers conceptualize and orient to place can influence linguistic productions. Additionally, places can and do have myriad meanings – some of which strongly contested. Furthermore, place is not static, as people move and the ideologies regarding certain places evolve over time. Authors probe these themes in this Element. It begins by reviewing the existing work on language & place within the field of sociolinguistics according to key themes in the literature – place orientation, gentrification, globalization, and commodification, amongst others. It also introduces key concepts and frameworks for studying place within allied fields such as geography, sociology, architecture, and psychology. Each author then presents a case study of language and place within their respective field sites: rural Appalachia and Greater New Orleans. The Element concludes by identifying areas for future development of place theory within sociolinguistics. This title is also available as Open Access on Cambridge Core.

This Element also has a video abstract: www.cambridge.org/Carmichael

Keywords: New Orleans, Appalachia, place attachment, sociolinguistics, sense of place

© Katie Carmichael and Paul E. Reed 2025

ISBNs: 9781009517287 (HB), 9781009380867 (PB), 9781009380874 (OC)
ISSNs: 2754-5539 (online), 2754-5520 (print)

Contents

1 Introduction   1

2 How We Got Here   2

3 Place in Sociolinguistics   4

4 Place in Allied Fields   24

5 The View from the Periphery: Agency, Authenticity, and Place Orientation in Post-Katrina Greater New Orleans   38

6 The Evocation of a Stigmatized Place: Hollering the Holler   63

7 Urban or Rural, Rooted or *Un*rooted, What's Local Is Local: Summarizing Case Study Themes   82

8 Conclusions and Future Directions   84

References   88

Language and Place 1

> Speech is a component of the total force that transforms nature into a human place.
> — (Tuan 1991: 685)

1 Introduction

It could be the taste of your favorite local dish; the smell of a flower that is native to your region; the sight of your city's skyline; or the sound of your hometown accent – myriad components play into one's sense of place, as humans by nature find meaning in and connection to our surroundings. As the descriptions demonstrate, our experiences of the places we live and move through are, by definition, subjective and sensory, and can feel deeply personal. Indeed, our sense of *self* is often profoundly influenced by the places we feel connected to (Proshansky, Fabian, & Kaminoff 1983). That said, sense of place is not solely an individualistic enterprise; our ideas about place identity are also co-constructed in interactions with others (Basso 1996a, 1996b), as we develop and point to ideologies about place, hierarchies of place, types of places, and so on. Language plays a significant role in these processes. One way language comes into play is via discursive constructions of place, which happen via talk about places (e.g., Modan 2007; Grieser 2022). More abstractly, a way of speaking may become associated with the place it is spoken, with indexical links evoking a sense of place upon hearing the dialect spoken there; and in a similar fashion, thinking of a place can bring to mind the local soundscape, including the accent. Johnstone & Kiesling (2008) argue that invoking a place means necessarily implicating ways of speaking tied to it, writing, "places and dialects are essentially linked (every place has a dialect; knowing a place means knowing its dialect)" (p. 6). In some communities, speakers agentively exploit this link, employing locally salient linguistic features in symbolic ways to express a place-based identity (Johnstone, Andrus, & Danielson 2006; Reed 2018a; Carmichael 2023).

Language *varieties* are inherently place-linked in part because language *users* are always *emplaced*, but also because the development of differentiating languages and dialects is often related to physical aspects of the landscape (settlement patterns; historical movements of people along common routes of travel; physical barriers between speakers such as oceans, rivers, mountains, and so on). Furthermore, sociolinguistic considerations of how a linguistic innovation might spread often consider speakers' movements across space – and the potential limitations that physical barriers as well as imagined (cf. Anderson 2006) borders might place on that diffusion across speech communities. Lastly, as sociolinguists in the third wave broach a growing interest in agency and performance of identity (cf. Eckert 2012), we have found that every identity factor – from ethnicity, to gender, to sexuality, to social class – has instantiations and social values specific to speakers' home communities. That is, these sign systems cannot be understood without a local, emplaced understanding of their significance in that specific social landscape. Thus, as sociolinguists, we are inherently working with language and place; in this Element, we encourage more in-depth engagement with place theory, in order to improve our *linguistic* theories about language variation and change. We further urge linguists to consider what our research can contribute more broadly to theorizations of place across fields.

As theories of place are becoming more commonly explored in studies of identity, it grows all the more important to better understand the relationship between place-linked ideologies and the sign systems used to express them (whether linguistic, visual, or otherwise). In this Element, we provide a roadmap of the ways sociolinguistics has thus far engaged with the concept of *place*,[1] from the inception of linguistic inquiry up through contemporary research, noting key readings in the sociolinguistics of place as well as notable intersections with other essential questions in the field. We then pull in interdisciplinary perspectives on *place* as it is studied in allied fields such as geography, psychology, sociology, anthropology, and architecture, identifying areas of place theory – as these fields understand it – that inherently impact identity and interaction. In this way, we draw attention to components of place theory that warrant deeper consideration by the field of sociolinguistics. To demonstrate how the tools of place theory can strengthen our sociolinguistic analyses within very different settings, we present two case studies on language and place: one in Greater New Orleans, and the other in rural Appalachia. We end by suggesting critical questions for the field of sociolinguistics moving forward, and ways that considerations of *place* can help provide essential insights toward answering these questions.

2 How We Got Here

As researchers interested in the sociolinguistics of place, we have similar questions about the relationship between language and place. Our paths to get here, however, differ widely, and we share them here to state our positionality and identify the individual lens we each bring to this work.

Katie was born in New Orleans (which she describes as "the placeyest place") but moved to Northern Virginia as an infant. Growing up in the DC suburbs – a land of strip malls, chain restaurants, big box retail, and McMansions – Katie

---

[1] Throughout this Element, when referring to 'place' as a concept – which may encapsulate many aspects of place, including but not limited to 'sense of place,' 'place identity,' 'place orientation,' 'place theory,' and so on – we will italicize the term.

felt a deep sense of disconnect with her hometown. What made Northern Virginia any different from any other suburb in the United States? It had no distinctive cuisine, no regionally specific culture or music to speak of, and most devastatingly to a budding linguist: no identifiably local way of speaking (this being due to a large transplant and short-term resident population, thanks to DC's status as a military and political destination, which has ultimately led to significant dialect leveling in the region). Katie returned to New Orleans for college, immersing herself in the magic of the food, music, culture, and language practices of her birthplace. Right in the middle of her undergraduate experience, however, Hurricane Katrina struck and changed everything. Many locals were permanently displaced, and new arrivals from elsewhere took their place. Still today, the city continues to evolve and to battle about what it means to be a 'true' New Orleanian, which Katie has noted commonly includes specific linguistic features – especially those which transplants could not authentically acquire or perform. To understand this linguistic battleground, Katie needed theoretical backing for how to analyze the performance of place identity, linguistic and otherwise, in post-Katrina New Orleans.

Paul, in contrast, grew up on a family farm in a small, rural town in Upper East Tennessee – a self-described 'educated hillbilly.' His family had been in the area for generations, and he grew up with the stories about kinfolk and local areas, literally heard at his parents' and grandparents' knees on the front porch of the homeplace. Home was a place of hollers, valleys, rivers, mountains, and a particular way of speaking that people noticed, locals and non-locals alike. Because of its location in the mountains, and the impact of extractive capitalism, the area was seen as backwoods and backward, and early on Paul learned that outside folks looked down on his hometown, and some local folks did too. However, other locals, including his grandparents and parents, had an evident connection to the area and loved it deeply in spite of its issues. The area continues to engender both stigma and love, leaving and staying. Through his work, Paul noted that many linguistic features seemed to correlate with a speaker's relationship to place, and he needed a means to understand, and perhaps quantify, that relationship to place.

As every researcher has their own particular relationships to the places they live, work, and study, we encourage reflection of how that positionality might affect one's interpretation of patterns observed in their fieldsite, and the lens that it puts on their understanding of the social meaning of emplaced language practices.

In the following section, we turn to a discussion of the ways that *place* has been conceived of and mobilized within sociolinguistic research up to now. It is our hope to draw together certain threads of inquiry within sociolinguistics that may not, at the face of it, be considered part of a research agenda centering explicitly on place, but which we propose are part of a burgeoning sociolinguistics of place.

3 Place in Sociolinguistics

3.1 From Dialect Geography to Enregisterment: Conceptions of Place in Sociolinguistics over Time

From the earliest mentions of language in the ancient world, discussion of language usage that is constrained and defined by *place* abound. The 'father of linguistics' Pāṇini included regional variants in his descriptions of the Indian subcontinent circa 400 BCE. Yang Xiong, an ancient Chinese grammarian, circa 200 BCE, identified and described regional and place-based variants in production (Yang & Asher 1995). The influence of *place* was included in much of the language scholarship from the early to late Middle Ages, from the Greco-Roman notations of regional variation in Latin by Sextus Empiricus in 400 CE to the Arabian Peninsula circa 800 CE where grammarians sought productions from rural tribespeople to document differences in their speech from that of speakers from urban areas.

As research shifted from the Middle Ages to the Modern Age, the impact of *place* on the study of language became more systematic and scientific, and researchers noted that place-based heterogeneity was the rule, seeking to show where and how the people in different areas spoke. Indeed, the output of such projects is generally called a Linguistic Atlas and quite literally mapped variation onto geographic locales, noting the ways language varied across space. The nineteenth century in particular saw a boom in the development of such studies, which students in linguistics learn via the romantic tales of Jules Gilliéron and Edmond Edmont biking through the French and Swiss countryside collecting data via use of dialect surveys and phonetic notation, and of Georg Wenker sending postcards across Germany to map pronunciation differences. In the 1930s, Hans Kurath began work on linguistic atlases of various regional US English varieties (Kurath 1939), followed up in the 1960s by Fred Cassidy and Joan Houston Hall's work with the *Dictionary of Regional American English* (DARE) (Cassidy & Houston Hall 1985–2013) and finally in the 2000s with William Labov, Sharon Ash, and Charles Boberg's *Atlas of North American English* (Labov, Ash, & Boberg 2006). Work in this tradition in the US continues with the Linguistic Atlas Project, now housed at the University of Kentucky (https://linguisticatlasproject.org/). In Europe, a number of significant Atlas projects started in the 1950s–60s, including the *Linguistic Atlas of England* (Orton 1960–1980) (with the notable recent updated account from MacKenzie, Bailey, & Turton 2022), *The Linguistic*

Atlas and Survey of Irish Dialects (LASID; Wagner 1958–1969), and the *Sprachatlas der deutschen Schweiz* (Hotzenköcherle et al. 1969–1997).

In the 1960s–70s, variationist sociolinguistics began to distinguish itself from dialectology in both methods used and questions posed. That said, in what is arguably the singular study that launched this line of inquiry, Labov's (1963) master's thesis on Martha's Vineyard, *place* played a key role. In this study, Labov demonstrated that how a speaker felt about the island (i.e., their place identity) affected how centralized the onglides of /ay/ and /aw/ were. Those speakers who used centralized variants were socially oriented to the island and its traditional way of life and expressed a desire to stay on the island. The vocalic production was a signal of the island, as Labov (1963: 304) writes, "it is apparent that the immediate meaning of this phonetic feature is 'Vineyarder'." Thus, from the very earliest work in the variationist tradition, place identity was central to interpreting the results.

Other early research in sociolinguistic variation shifted to cities, such as New York City (Labov 1966), Detroit (Wolfram 1969), Panama City (Cedergren 1973), Norwich (Trudgill 1974), and Belfast (Milroy & Milroy 1978). In these urban contexts, the population density put speakers in daily contact with people who were very much not like them on a number of social axes – in contrast to a prior focus on Non-Mobile Old Rural Men (or NORMs). In these studies, place was held 'constant' in a sense, allowing for an in-depth examination of other social factors such as gender, ethnicity, social class, and so on. Assumptions of non-mobility were indeed built into the idea of speech communities, with one of the most cited definitions being from Labov (1972: 120–121), who wrote that "the speech community is not defined by any marked agreement in the use of language elements, so much as by participation in a set of shared norms; these norms may be observed in overt types of evaluative behavior, and by the uniformity of abstract patterns of variation which are invariant in respect to particular levels of usage." As one delves into who fits this definition, mobile speakers and those who did not have two parents from an area could be excluded, as they may not share the exact same norms. This approach has limited the scope of what and who counted as authentic speakers, with a number of researchers (e.g., Bucholtz 2003; Eckert 2004; Coupland 2010) critiquing the ways sociolinguists and community members alike define authentic speaker status. In fact, the inclusion criteria in Labov's early work were so stringent that Kerswill (1993) noted these methods ultimately excluded almost 50 percent of NYC residents who lived in the area where the research was conducted.

In an increasingly mobile and globalized world, there is more reason than ever to revisit the methodological assumption of what Britain (2016) called 'sedentarism.' Crucially, in his critique of sedentarism in sociolinguistic research, Britain draws from work on mobility from human geography, demonstrating a key example of how considering *place* from a theoretical standpoint can improve upon all manner of conclusions we draw from the data we deem acceptable, appropriate, and authentic. Blommaert (2016) follows this thread beyond considerations of dialectal diversity to examine questions of superdiversity, globalization, and multilingualism in 'macro-sociolinguistics,' writing, "migration as a force behind multilingualism compels analysts to consider mobile people – people who do not stay in the place where their languages are traditionally used, to put it simply – whose linguistic resources and communicative opportunities are affected by such forms of mobility" (p. 245). And there is every reason to consider mobility itself as a force on sociolinguistic variation, even in monolingual contexts. Mobility can, for example, affect social network ties, as Milroy & Milroy (1978) argue in Belfast, in which the speakers who traveled more for work or other reasons often had looser network ties; since dense, multiplex networks tend to have a conserving effect, there are clear implications for linguistic change tied to speaker mobility within this framework. Similarly, in Brasilia, Bortini-Ricardo (1985) evaluated rural individuals who moved to the urban area, finding that the social network of the speaker was key to understanding any change in the rural vernacular (what she calls the 'diffuseness' of dialect features). This was also mediated via the gender of the speaker – which was more related to the public/private sphere as men tended to work outside the home. More recently, Stanford (2006, 2009) shows the durability of dialect features amongst the Sui people of Southwest China in relation to their social networks. Cultural practices in this region prescribe cross-clan (and thus cross-dialectal) marriages, and wives tend to maintain the characteristic features of their home dialects – even after decades of living in other places.

Furthermore, as we consider the movements of people, we might investigate why certain groups maintain and/or develop varieties linked to places where they are no longer located. In her work on the Jewish diaspora, Benor (2010) addresses this via the notion of 'ethnolinguistic repertoire,' which can help a researcher understand the impact of "ancestral migrations, activities, ideologies, allegiances, contacts with other groups, boundaries between insiders and outsiders" as well as permitting us to "explore how a group's repertoire crystallizes, often after migration or colonization" (161). That is, such repertoires both point to *another place*, and point to the ways that our linguistic practices tied to that place might be viewed as *out-of-place* in this new context, and thus may require monitoring and adjustment based on audience.

The other side of the coin on the question of mobility is that of *immobility* or rootedness. Reed (2018a, 2020a, inter alia) has written extensively on the topic of rootedness. In his research, speakers from a small, rural town in Tennessee had varying levels of attachment to place – measured via a rootedness score – even though they all lived (and had lived) there most of their lives. Rootedness was predictive of many linguistic patterns in the community, including features explicitly commented upon in the community and those below the level of consciousness. Many populations that are deeply rooted in place are isolated from external mobile populations in some way – whether that isolation is social, geographic, or otherwise. A prime example of how this can affect linguistic practices comes from island populations, such as Ocracoke (Wolfram 1997) and Smith Island (Schilling 2017) in the United States, and in a more extreme case, in the island of Tristan da Cunha (Schreier 2010), the most remote island in the world with a unique dialect of English spoken by its inhabitants. Trudgill (2020) argues that "conservative language varieties tend generally to be those which are relatively more geographically isolated, as well as relatively more stable socially, than more innovating language varieties," illustrating this trend across dozens of languages spanning hundreds of years of language change and social upheaval. The tie between language and place can also be observed in the case of the inverse situation: a place changing, and the language changing along with it. Bailey et al. (1996) document this trend in post–World War II Texas and Oklahoma, demonstrating that the rapid and dramatic population changes during this time period led to 'catastrophic' language change; that is, rapid demographic and linguistic change in tandem.

More recently, sociolinguistics has arguably seen a 'place turn,' in no small part ushered in via Barbara Johnstone's critical work at the intersection of linguistic anthropology and sociolinguistics (e.g., Johnstone 2004, 2009, 2010a, 2010b). Much of this work has centered on language spoken in Pittsburgh, Pennsylvania – a mid-sized rust belt city in the United States. Similar to Bailey et al. (1996), Johnstone, Andrus, & Danielson (2006) document how demographic changes via post–World War II in-migration to this previously rather isolated town over the twentieth century changed the metapragmatic awareness in Pittsburgh. Mobilizing Silverstein's (2003) orders of indexicality alongside Labov's (1972) indicators, markers, and stereotypes, Johnstone et al. argued that this contact between outsiders and local Pittsburgh residents led to greater awareness of locally marked linguistic features, predominantly used by working-class Pittsburgh residents. Over time, this dialect – referred to locally as "Pittsburghese" – underwent the process of *enregisterment* (Agha 2003), or reification as "The Pittsburgh Dialect." In the process, the most salient features became divorced from their original context of users and available for performance – for example, in Pittsburghese, the monophthongization of /aw/ in words like "dahntahn" became a shibboleth of local authenticity. In this analysis, Johnstone provides key frameworks and tools for understanding the ways place-linked linguistic features develop these associations, walking readers through the path of development from first-order indexicality wherein listeners notice regional variants and associate them with basic sociodemographic categories with which they are correlated (in this case, working class speakers from Southwest Pennsylvania), second-order indexicality in which the feature becomes available for social work via stylistic variation, and finally third-order indexicality in which local features may be agentively performed in order to index a Pittsburghese identity (Johnstone, Andrus, & Danielson 2006: 82).

In following with this place turn, a number of edited volumes have appeared over the past decade addressing these key questions about the sociolinguistics of place. Montgomery and Moore's (2017) *Language and a Sense of Place* brings together scholars across linguistic disciplines, showing how various approaches can better incorporate and discuss *place*, particularly sense of place. And in Cornips and de Rooij's (2018) *The Sociolinguistics of Place and Belonging: Perspectives from the Margins*, linguistic scholars discuss how place and belonging have varied effects in cities versus areas on the 'margins.' By focusing on places 'at the margin,' the authors in this book highlight how *place* and its meanings are continually discussed, negotiated, and renegotiated. Such collections demonstrate how critical it is to continue to interrogate *place* from a broad sociolinguistic perspective.

We would additionally argue that recent conversations about the decolonization of linguistics (e.g., Charity Hudley, Mallinson, & Bucholtz 2024) have by their very nature a relationship with place. To begin with, some of the colonial practices that these authors rightfully call out have everything to do with linguists staking claim to a specific community, and its associated language, and imposing out-of-place standards or viewpoints on them; moreover, this hierarchical consideration of *place* – whereby some places 'dominate' or preempt others – influence how dwellers around the globe see and position these places in their own mental schemas, as well as how we as researchers see and organize them (see, e.g., conversations about The Global North/South within linguistics as well as other fields). Indeed, Braithewaite & Ali (2024: 64) assert, "attempts to decolonize the academic field of linguistics must grapple with the colonial geography of the field: the ways in which power and opportunity are concentrated in certain parts of the world, the ways that data is extracted from other parts of the world, and the ways that such factors shape the lives of linguists from different parts of the world, and the field as a whole. Notions of core and periphery within the field of linguistics are surely tied to geographical cores and peripheries." That is, the very considerations we exhort deeper reflection upon within our analyses might be just as fruitfully turned inward on our practices as researchers.

3.2 Physicality of Place and Space: Linguistic Landscapes and Language Commodification

While a number of sociolinguistic studies consider *place* as a potential explanatory factor for linguistic practices observed, yet other studies treat *place* as the data itself, asking what we can learn about language (and language ideologies) from the physical landscape and related artifacts.

Engaging directly with the physicality of space, research on linguistic landscapes and geosemiotics note the way that linguistic symbols surround us, contributing to our sense of place while also impacting – at times even policing – our movement across space. Landry & Bourhis (1997) introduce the concept of linguistic landscape by examining ideologies and usage of French and English across Canada, and its correlation to the (literal) visibility of these languages. In doing so, they documented the ways that language policy (in the form of signage) and language ideologies crucially interact and affect linguistic vitality. Perhaps unsurprisingly given these origins, some of the most compelling work on linguistic landscapes takes place in multilingual communities – for example, in Singapore (Hult & Kelly-Holmes 2019; Tang 2020), Ireland (Kallen 2011; Moriarty 2014), or Israel (Horesh & Gafter 2022) – or in diaspora communities – for example, Washington D.C.'s Chinatown (e.g., Leeman & Modan 2010; Lou 2016). In this work, the visual presence of a given language in signage has often been interpreted as institutional support for that language, examined in frameworks of dominance, power, and policy; attention has also been given to the ways that cultural and linguistic erasure in a given landscape can reflect marginalization of certain groups in these spaces.

In her various work on language, commodification and globalization (e.g., Heller 2003, 2010; Duchêne & Heller 2012), Monica Heller has pointed to the ways that language can index certain nationalities to be sure, but also the evaluations associated with those place-based identities. These in turn can in a capitalistic society come to be assigned a literal monetary value. In Canada, when it comes to use of English or French, Heller (2003: 475) writes that "tensions between commodity and authenticity [become] sites of struggle over who gets to define what counts as a legitimate identity, or what counts as an excellent product." One way that linguistic commodification comes to be explicitly tied to place is via tourism. In an analysis of Pittsburghese words and phrases on Tee-shirts and other merchandise, Johnstone (2009) notes how locals could literally purchase and wear the ways of speaking that had come to be associated with an authentic Pittsburgh identity – regardless of whether they themselves used these features. Hall-Lew, Fairs, & Lew (2015) further demonstrate how 'light' Scottish accents were valued in tourism in Edinburgh, Scotland as a marker of authenticity and ties to the local place, whereas 'heavier' accents were disvalued and viewed as unintelligible to outsiders. Remlinger (2018) has analyzed the effect of tourism and enregisterment in the Upper Peninsula of Michigan in the United States, showing how commercialization, as well as local cultural pride, drives how residents commodify and discuss place. Linguistic commodification can also be literally embedded into the physical landscape, as Jaffe (2019) examines in the case of touristic monetization of minority language Corsican; Jaffe described a small town in which the tourism board installed QR codes linking Corsican language and music to specific locations, creating a linkage between pride and profit.

3.3 Defining a Locale: Place Identity and Sense of Place

We have established that places can be meaningful, and language is one tool humans have to express their understandings of the world around them. By using language to name places, or talk about them, speakers may transform a geographic entity to a social one (Tuan 1991). Crucially, though, one's ideas about a place's identity may not align with another's in the community, or the place itself may change over time, with *talk about place* sometimes providing key insight into how residents see these places, and see their role in place-making. Additionally, considering how individuals view, discuss, and understand a place helps researchers to heed the call made by Auer (2013), who discusses some of the shortcomings of research that views space and place as 'containers' of people, with an identical and inalienable influence on all speakers at all times. Instead, Auer proposes that research on language and place reverse this approach and instead view speakers "as agents who choose variables from a range of options as a way of "placing" themselves, and enabling their recipients to "place" them" (p. 15).

Linguistic anthropology and studies of indigeneity in linguistics have long understood the significance of *place* within linguistic and cultural systems. Basso (1996b: 85) writes, "[f]ueled by sentiments of inclusion, belonging, and connectedness to the past, sense of place roots individuals in the social and cultural soils from which they have sprung together, holding them there in the grip of a shared identity, a localized version of selfhood." That is – our homeplace is central to our personal identity, and in the formulation of our social reality and cultural norms. As these homeplaces have been unjustly stripped away from indigenous groups, reclaiming their terrain has been central to the reclamation process. One way this is enacted is via reinstatement of standard indigenous names for geographic entities such as mountains, volcanos, and towns. In her examination of linguistic and ecological sustainability in

Greenland, Grenoble (2011: 28) states that "identity and place are intrinsically linked." She goes on to provide examples of geographically specific terms essential to Kalaallisut lifestyles, demonstrating the essentially emplaced nature of language for this indigenous group. Grenoble argues that toponym restoration into Kalaalisut place names is central to the indigenous reclamation procedures ongoing in the country, as a way of reinstating Kalaallisut labels that had been erased by Danish colonizing terms. As Tuan (1991: 688) writes: "Naming is power – the creative power to call something into being, to render the invisible visible, to impart a certain character to things." Indeed, examination of toponyms themselves can provide significant context for the historical developments in a given region. In the Philippines, Lesho & Sippola (2018) document the use of Tagalog, Spanish, and English place names by varied groups, noting how the language and patterns of different place names reflected historical shifts in colonial and indigenous power over time. And Schiefflin (2018) in Papua New Guinea compares and contrasts Bonsavi children's and adults' place-naming and place-making, showing how the influence of missionary presence can change how residents discuss the place.

Places can also come to stand in for certain social types and stances, sometimes only legible to the people who move through these spaces. In a study of Western Apache narratives, Basso (1996a, 1996b) documents how places were used in stories told to admonish certain negatively viewed behaviors, contributing to a moral geography expressed via metaphor and narrative. Without an insider understanding of the mythology surrounding these places, the communication of intent in these stories remains opaque. Expanding this concept to the DC neighborhood of Mt. Pleasant, Modan (2007) examines discourse strategies used to construct narratives about the identity of Mt. Pleasant as a place. Modan noted how residents identified certain behaviors and residents as the focal center of the neighborhood, discursively locating those outside of these descriptions as peripheral nonmembers, thereby delegitimizing their claims to Mt. Pleasant. Such conflicts and contestations about the sense of a place are common. Blu (1996) found that in their discussion of local places, the Lumbee Indians of Robeson County, North Carolina focus on the social qualities of a place. In contrast, non-Lumbee residents, without the same historical ties to Robeson County as "homeland," are more likely to note visual or physical features of the landscape. Such findings demonstrate the multiplicity of place identities and the meanings of *place*, even within a single community.

A common site of contested place identity arises in the case of a place itself changing over time, in terms of its inhabitants or the physical structures thereabout. Gentrification offers a key example of such a place-shift. Gentrification is generally defined as processes of urban renewal or reinvestment in specific communities that increase property values, thereby pricing out many historic residents who are displaced in the process. Linguistic research on gentrifying spaces can provide insights into how the process of gentrification is unfolding, how it is perceived by longstanding residents as well as new arrivals, and how the demographic changes impact the language varieties traditionally linked to that place. For example, in the historically Black and rapidly gentrifying Washington, DC neighborhood of Anacostia, Grieser (2022) notes the way participants racialized gentrifiers as white, taking varied stances toward them in conversation. Regardless of personal stance, however, Grieser documents the strategies – via deictics, pronoun usage, and erasure (Irvine & Gal 2000) – all participants used to construct a specifically Black Anacostia, in which white DC residents were marked in terms of race, place, and class. We see in these examples that place comes to stand in for much more complex concepts than one's personal identification – that talk about *place* is a proxy for talk about taboo behaviors or identities in a given community. Ilbury (2021) demonstrates these processes via discursive analysis of East Londoners' descriptions of places, and the people – and ways of speaking – linked to them, wherein they circumscribe who and what belongs where. Such questions of 'claim to place' also resonate in Regan's (2022) work highlighting the conflict in Texas between newcomers versus longstanding locals, who differed in notable ways in their pronunciations of street names in the city of Austin, which Regan argues indexed locally salient identities. These connections between places and ideologies exist already in any community; it is crucial to understand the ways that these beliefs are mobilized in interaction to create a taxonomy of belonging – to identify where one fits into the surrounding landscape, and who ought to be excluded from conceptions of what that place means.

Gentrification can also affect specific speech patterns, in the case of place-linked features. Grieser (2022) examines this question in terms of a dialect density measure for African American Language (AAL) features, noting that the highest rates occur in discussions of change, race, and Washington, DC; Grieser argues that participants are making iconic use of AAL features to construct DC as a "Black place," in contrast with the perceived whiteness of gentrification and change that the neighborhood is undergoing. Similarly, Becker (2009) analyzes nonrhoticity, an iconically NYC feature, in the gentrifying neighborhood of the Lower East Side, finding that residents increased their rates of nonrhoticity when talking about neighborhood-related topics. As gentrification expands in urban areas around the world, it will become essential to pose questions about the effects on language usage – not just the obvious effects relating to demographic change within a locale, but also changes to a given place identity, and to the ways in which residents orient to the places they live.

3.4 Globalization, Mobility, and Migration in Sociolinguistics

Over the past twenty years, sociolinguistics has also arguably seen what Pienimäki, Väisänen, & Hiippala (2024: 5) term a 'mobilities turn,' taking us from what Britain (2016: 217) calls a 'sedentarist' view of language to a deeper engagement with and understanding of the forces of movement on modern society. Crucial to many of these insights has been Jan Blommaert's pioneering work (e.g., Dong & Blommaert 2009; Blommaert 2016) considering questions of place, time, and scale as he examined migrant communities in a distinctly international context. Indeed, Blommaert & Rampton (2011: 3) write, "[r]ather than working with homogeneity, stability and boundedness as the starting assumptions, mobility, mixing, political dynamics and historical embedding are now central concerns in the study of languages, language groups and communication." As Kerswill (2006) points out: migration necessarily has sociolinguistic consequences for the home community, the recipient community, and of course for the migrants themselves. And of course, every context of migration is different, and the experience of each migrant – and their resulting orientations toward new and old homes – will also be unique (cf. Hua 2017).

Globalization is a key consideration in current-day examinations of language and place, though its effects are not simple to characterize, in part because they are not consistent across communities. Rather, they depend on myriad social, political, and linguistic forces. Schilling (2017: 178) writes:

> The assertion of localness in the face of homogenizing forces is also a pervasive theme in studies of language and globalization, and often the result of cultural and linguistic contact is neither the erasure of local norms or the replacement of local forms with features in wider usage, but rather the creation of hybrid, "glocalized" linguistic and social practices.

Any sociolinguist who has interacted with journalists or the general public recently can attest to this general worry over linguistic homogenization across space, and the ways individuals push back on these forces via emphasis on their local uniqueness.

We can also consider the ways language is impacted by borders and 'imagined communities' (Anderson 2006) based on nationality and region. Park & Wee (2017) describe in detail the relationship between a nation-state and language, and the ways that transnationalism challenges that relationship by decoupling the mythical, relatively recent trope of a 1:1 ratio between language and nation. They stress the significance of the different forms of social capital that varied languages – and language users – may embody. Indeed, the status of a language user in a given locale can depend on the social value of their identity and how this frames the presence of their language usage in a new space. We could consider, for example, the difference between the labels *refugee, asylum seeker, migrant worker, illegal alien, immigrant, mobile worker, jetsetter,* and *ex-pat* and the raced, classed, and otherwise socially value-laden associations with each of these. Indeed, we echo that essential to any work on mobility is the awareness that not all movement across space is the same; migration may be voluntary versus involuntary – resulting in drastically different relationships with new and old homes (cf. Cotter & Horesh 2015).

Mobility across national and linguistic borders brings with it questions of language contact; myriad social factors come into play in these contexts, affecting whether heritage languages are retained or lost and whether new dialects (koines) or mixed codes (pidgins, Creoles) arise (cf. Polinsky 2018; Hickey 2020; inter alia). Tseng & Hinrichs (2021) introduced the concept of *diaspora sociolinguistics*, pointing out that this approach offers a bridge between questions of heritage languages and immigration, and those developments that occur in the generations to come, as previously newcomer populations take root and establish a new sense of identity in the place they have built their communities.

These demographic changes, both international and intranational, can also have impacts on the 'founder dialect' in a given region (Mufwene 2001), as Tillery, Bailey, & Wikle (2004) illustrate in Texas and Oklahoma given large scale migration in and out of these regions following World War II. Principally, Tillery et al. show that urbanization and metropolitanization had key linguistic impacts, and what had been described previously as regional variations were now better described as metropolitan/nonmetropolitan variation. Relatedly, Trudgill et al. (2000) demonstrate that researchers may use details about migrating speakers' dialects – and the relative proportions of variants therein – to make predictions about how dialect features are transmitted across generations. Labov's (2007) classic *Transmission and Diffusion* paper provides further tools for the consideration of how linguistic features are transmitted within a community and diffused across space with migration of speakers from one locale to another. Labov noted structural differences in patterns associated with the spread of linguistic changes, suggesting this might be due to the differences in learning by children (transmission) versus adults (diffusion). Thus, some nuances of patterns will be transmitted locally, but these same nuances may not diffuse across communities. Recent work on African American Language (AAL) considering the key role of the Great Migration of African Americans in the United States in shaping the linguistic features found in the varieties of AAL spoken in Northern US areas has also confronted these key issues of demographic change and linguistic diffusion (Farrington 2019). Farrington notes that some features associated with AAL 'intensified' over time, that is, increased in frequency in the speech of more speakers and occurred across a wider geographic area. However, the local community dynamics (North/South, urban/rural) played a pivotal role in the spread and diffusion of consonantal features. Notably, these studies frame their questions to be about language change across space, though there is very little consideration about speakers' stances toward their home dialect, versus the dialects they encounter in their new homes. And indeed, one's home, or sense of belonging, may not be limited to one geographic location or community.

One way we can see the impacts of a speaker-oriented approach to these questions is via second dialect acquisition studies. Nycz (2015) provides a helpful summary of the work in this realm, drawing attention to how some researchers have considered second dialect acquisition as a subtype of accommodation (with Trudgill (1986) using the phrase "long-term accommodation"). Work in this domain raises crucial questions for how to think about the processes inherent in dialect contact, acquisition, and leveling both at the individual level and the community level. In their analysis of the "new town" planned community of Milton Keynes, Kerswill & Williams (2000) extended concepts from language contact (e.g., Mesthrie 1993) to consideration of dialect contact and dialect leveling. They argue that the dialect developing in this town was the result of koinézation between incoming varieties of English. Kerswill & Williams identify key factors to consider in such contexts, such as the population coming from different dialect groups, the proportion of children to adults in the community, the degree of contact (and social motivations to expand social networks beyond those who are from one's dialect region of origin), and the time depth/suddenness of contact. Evans (2004) elaborates upon this in her work on Appalachian migrants in Michigan, noting a correlation between the strength of the Appalachian social network with the acquisition (or not) of the raised /æ/ of the local Ypsilanti, Michigan dialect. Furthermore, Jones (2003) shows how speakers can both accommodate to local varieties (in her studies, adopting Northern Cities Vowel-shifted front vowels) but also retain features to differentiate (here, maintaining fronted back vowels common in Southern US dialects).

Within some recent studies on speaker mobility, place orientation has proven to be a key predictor of linguistic variation, as researchers probe the role of speaker attachment to new and old homeplaces in the adoption/retention of dialectal features linked to these locales. In New Orleans, Carmichael (2017) compares New Orleanians permanently displaced after Hurricane Katrina to those who returned to their pre-Katrina homes, finding no significant difference in nonrhoticity rates between groups; however, those most oriented toward their pre-Katrina homes – whether or not they relocated – were those most nonrhotic. Adopting a similar place orientation scale, Nycz (2019) found that in the case of

Canadian English speakers living in New York City, age of arrival and years spent in NYC do not significantly predict the distinction between COT and CAUGHT realizations, though orientation toward NYC does. Beaman (2021) documents similar patterns in use of Swabian German, where she developed calculations of both Swabian orientation and mobility within and without the region; with longitudinal data, she was able to track the ways that increasing mobility across space as well as decreasing orientation to a Swabian-specific identity over time has led to reduced usage of marked Swabian features and overall increased dialect leveling in southwest Germany. Considering the question of mobility in the case of Swiss German, Steiner et al. (2023) have demonstrated the other side of this coin, noting the ways that tight-knit social networks and a strong sense of local identity contribute to the conservation of traditional linguistic features.

3.5 Perceptual Approaches to Language and Place

While most of the studies described earlier represent production studies, examining how individuals produce language, it is also crucial to understand perception – especially social perception – of place-linked language. Pioneering work in this area has come from perceptual dialectology, which examines folk understandings of language variation; one of the most famous tasks in this tradition asks participants to mark on a blank map "where people speak differently," and then to list and/or rank the qualities of those places and/or those speakers. Resulting perceptual dialectology maps demonstrate how listeners *perceive* the accents and dialects of those around them, and also what they tend to *believe* about speakers from those areas. The earliest work on folk perceptions of regional accents took place in the Netherlands (Rensink 1955) and Japan (Grootaers 1959), centering on participants' perception of 'degree of difference' between regional dialects. Expanding on this work, Preston's (1989, 1999) studies in the United States ask more pointed questions about the *social* associations of regional American accents. Notably, he found that while Michiganders described their own speech patterns as relatively unaccented, pleasant, and 'normal,' they viewed Alabamians' speech as accented, unpleasant, and stigmatized. What is particularly illuminating is that Alabamians themselves tended to share some of the same stigmas for their own speech, what has been termed 'linguistic insecurity,' where speakers believe that the "variety they use is somehow inferior, ugly, or bad" (Meyerhoff 2006: 292). More recently, the development of Geographic Information System (GIS) tools has provided opportunities for uncovering finer-grained distinctions and for aggregating larger quantities of data more efficiently (Montgomery & Stoeckle 2013; Montgomery 2017). Moreover, increasingly work on perceptual dialectology probes the question of scale, examining place-based folk perceptions in individual states or regions – for example, Ohio (Benson 2003); California (Bucholtz et al. 2007); Washington (Evans 2013, 2016); the island of O'ahu in Hawai'i (Drager & Grama 2014); New England (Jones 2015); Kentucky (Cramer 2016) – and even within a single city – for example, Dublin (Lonergan 2016); Seoul (Jeon & Cukor-Avila 2016); Miami (Callesano 2020); and New Orleans (Dajko & Carmichael 2023). Recent edited collections and summary articles about perceptual dialectology and 'language regard' (e.g., Cramer & Montgomery 2016; Evans, Benson, & Stanford 2018; Cramer 2021) illustrate how sociolinguistic perceptions intersect with beliefs about different places around the world, and how folk linguistic methods can uncover these connections.

Beyond map-drawing, perceptual experiments have also provided key insights into the relationship between language & place, in particular those centered on regional dialect classification and evaluation. For example, in a series of US English dialect classification tasks, Clopper & Pisoni (2004, 2006, 2007) have demonstrated that not only can listeners often correctly identify the regional origin of speakers, but that more mobile listeners feature higher accuracy in their classifications, which Clopper & Pisoni attribute to greater experience with diverse regional dialects. In this series of studies, audio clips of speakers from throughout the United States were presented to naive listeners, who completed a forced-choice task to classify the suspected region of the listener. Using similar methods, Ladegaard (1998) found that Danish listeners held such strong sociolinguistic stereotypes about different national/regional varieties of English (American English, Australian English, and three types of British English – Received Pronunciation, Cockney, and Scottish English) that even if individual listeners could not identify the place of origin of the speaker, they still accurately identified the national stereotypes associated with the place based on audio clips of speakers from those places.

The level of control available for experimental perception work also allows for teasing apart the effects of specific linguistic and social cues. For example, van Bezooijen & Gooskens (1999) presented listeners from the Netherlands and the United Kingdom with audio recordings of different regional dialects in their home country, manipulating which levels of linguistic features were available: solely intonation (via low-pass filter), solely phonetic features (via monotonization of pitch across utterance), or the full speech signal; they found that for both languages, listeners were very accurate at identifying the regional origin of the recording in question and that they performed better with phonetic features than with prosody alone. In the United States, Plichta & Preston (2005) presented listeners with a gradient scale of /ai/-monophthongization and asked them to place the speaker in question along a North-to-South dimension in the United States. Although participants reported feeling incapable of adequately discriminating between /ai/ tokens, in general, the tokens were accurately placed on a North-to-South continuum. Plichta and Preston conclude that this accuracy demonstrated that listeners have access to significant implicit awareness of regional variation and the associated social associations of various regions.

At a similarly fine-grained level, research in sociophonetic perception has demonstrated that priming listeners with speaker origin affects their perception, categorization, and even production of speech sounds. Famously, Niedzielski (1999) has shown that Detroit listeners categorize tokens of /aw/ as more raised when they are told that the speaker was from Canada versus Detroit, due to ideologies linking /aw/-raising to Canadian speech. This effect was expanded upon in New Zealand with both explicit and implicit priming of place, as Kiwi participants produced more Australian-like vowels when the word 'Australia' appeared at the top of their answer sheet (Hay, Nolan, & Drager 2006), and categorized vowels they heard as more Australian when a stuffed kangaroo and koala (animals iconically associated with Australia) were merely present in the experimenting site (Hay & Drager 2010). Wade, Embick, & Tamminga (2023) further emphasize the significance of place-linked linguistic expectations via a task in which US listeners were primed with regional origin – either within the American South or the Midwest – then heard a speaker from the opposite region, producing mismatch between the locale and the accent presented. Participants were then recorded speaking, and their 'convergence' toward Southern features were examined. Both the 'Southern' label and the Southern acoustic cues triggered convergence, with Southern participants notably converging more in response to the acoustic cues and non-Southerners converging more in response to the Southern label, interpreted as a result of their 'out-group' stereotyped perceptions of what a Southerner sounds like.

Information about the regional origin of a speaker can also influence listeners' social evaluations of those speakers. For example, in a matched guise test examining social judgments of speakers using the alveolar versus velar variant of (ING), Campbell-Kibler (2009) shows that American English speakers who used the alveolar variant of (ING) were down-rated on intelligence *unless* they were also heard as Southern; based on qualitative analysis of follow-up interviews, she concludes that because alveolar (ING) was expected from Southerners, they were not down-rated on social qualities when using this otherwise stigmatized feature. Carmichael (2018) similarly found that within the US, Southerners heard as 'more accented' in a listening task were *less* down-rated on status and solidarity ratings compared to 'more accented' New Yorkers and Midwesterners; she argues this is due to an expectation of accentedness from Southerners which creates allowances for their accented speech. In both cases, place-based expectations specifically for Southern US speakers affect how listeners respond to the stimuli.

3.6 Contemporary Methods in Measuring Place Orientation in Sociolinguistics

A significant contemporary question in sociolinguistics is: how do we account for speakers' varying relationships to their home(s) in examinations of their language practices? The evidence for the influence of *place* is clear, longstanding, and pervasive, and yet, we also see that not every person from a particular place sounds alike, nor do all speakers use features, or all features, that are associated with a certain place. Thus, researchers have utilized various methods to attempt to capture the difference in *place orientation* or the ways speakers might relate to varied places in which they have spent time. Within sociolinguistics this idea is not new; Labov's (1963) Martha's Vineyard study indeed centers the orientation of Islanders toward island norms versus external norms, and Eckert's (1989) classic 'jocks and burnouts' study – while generally interpreted as reflecting aspects of social class – features the clear influence of place orientation, with burnouts oriented toward local/urban norms and jocks oriented toward extralocal/suburban norms. These examples present a binary internal versus external orientation categorization; yet more recent research has attempted to capture place orientation in a multifaceted metric. In Table 1, we summarize some of the approaches that researchers have taken in this thread; the detailed descriptions of each method as represented in the original source material are presented in the Online Appendix.

A number of uniting trends can be observed in this table – for example, the physical residence of a speaker, their family, and their friends, as well as the location of a speaker's school and workplace – though these are often measured and weighted differently. Many researchers make use of questionnaires or weighted evaluations of demographic history. Some studies draw from discourse analysis, for example, Pabst's and Schoux Casey's use of themes from interviews; Pabst devised scoring based on these themes, while Schoux Casey categorizes speakers in her study of New Orleans English as either locally or externally oriented based on whether their discussion throughout interviews focused on New Orleans-specific themes or took a more national/global lens to discussion topics. Studies focused on attachment to a given place focus on time spent in that place (e.g., Reed 2016, 2020a), while those centered on mobility (e.g., Carmichael 2017, 2023; Beaman 2021) consider aspects of local allegiance and desire to relocate. Intriguingly, some measures include linguistic practices already established to be tied to place identity (e.g., Solomon [1999] which considered the relationship between codeswitching and the use of certain variants in Valladolíd, Mexico). There is no one-size-fits-all answer to how place orientation ought to be captured across locales, but identifying common predictors across different studies can improve our methods for measuring place orientation.

Table 1 Examples of place orientation metrics in sociolinguistic research

Study	Metric name	Location	Metric facets
Solomon (1999: 178–179)	Cosmopolitan Orientation	Valladolid, Yucatán, Mexico	Scored responses to questions related to: 1. Experience with and attitudes toward larger urban areas 2. Use of indigenous language in conversational settings
Chambers (2000: 180–181)	Regionality Index	Canada	1. Where the speaker was raised from 8 to 18 2. Where the speaker was born 3. Where the speaker lives now 4. Where the speaker's mother and father were born
Schoux Casey (2013: 76)	Local Orientation	New Orleans, Louisiana, United States	Discourse analysis approach – identified as locally oriented if: 1. "[P]rimarily brought up local topics through the lens of personal experience, and took a strong New Orleans-centric perspective across topics" 2. "[u]sed first person when speaking of the city as a whole" 3. "[S]pecifically discussed themselves as embodying New Orleanian-ness"
Reed (2016: 74–77, 2020a: 207–210)	Rootedness Score	East Tennessee United States	Weighted responses to questions related to: 1. Willingness to relocate 2. Travel habits 3. Self-identification with region 4. Familial connection 5. Areal identification ranking 6. Local integration 7. Centrality of place identity

Source	Index name	Location	Components
Carmichael (2017: 705, 2023: 6–7)	Extra-Chalmatian Orientation/Multi-dimensional Place Orientation Metric	Chalmette, Louisiana, United States	1. Identification as Chalmatian (locally multivalent identifier) 2. Desire to leave Chalmette 3. Residential history 4. Schooling location(s) 5. Workplace location(s)
Monka, Quist, & Skovse (2020: 6)	Index of Local Attachment	Denmark	1. Mother's geographical background 2. Father's geographical background 3. Places of residence 4. Places of schooling 5. Location of spare-time job 6. Location of leisure activity 7. Geographical location of friends 8. Future geographical prospects
Beaman (2021: 36–37)	Swabian Orientation	Swabia, Germany	Weighted responses to questions related to: 1. Swabian allegiance 2. Swabian language attitudes 3. Swabian cultural competence 4. Swabian language usage

Table 1 (cont.)

Study	Metric name	Location	Metric facets
Beaman (2021: 38–39)	Swabian Mobility Index	Swabia and Germany	1. Residential dispersion – number of moves a speaker makes in lifetime and years lived 2. Residential distance – number of kilometers from hometown for each move and years lived in each place
Pabst (2022: 129)	Local Affiliation Score	Aroostook County, Maine, United States	Qualitative themes shared by speakers during interviews 1. Description as hard-working 2. Past or present engagement in hunting 3. Past or present engagement in other outdoor activities 4. Description as down to earth, enjoying the simple things in life 5. Mention of the interviewee helping other people 6. Focus on positive aspects of local life and culture 7. Limited time living outside of Northern Maine
Jeszenszky, Steiner, & Leemann (2024)	Linguistic Mobility Index	Switzerland	Weighted (according to their own exposure, and their 'relational' exposure) scores for: 1. Mother's regional origin 2. Father's regional origin 3. Partner's regional origin 4. Place of education 5. Workplace 6. External residence (time spent living elsewhere)

3.7 Intersectionality: Place and Other Social Factors

Place identity can intersect in varied ways with other social factors. Since all speech is necessarily *emplaced*, it is perhaps unsurprising that there are particular localized instantiations of identities – combinations of social factors that produce specific place-linked types or personae (think, e.g., of the Beijing 'Smooth Operator' [Zhang 2008], the California Valley Girl [D'Onofrio 2015; Villarreal 2016], and the aloof New Yorker [Becker 2014], inter alia).

Racial, ethnic, and religious identity can vary across locales, and there can be specifically localized ways of 'sounding' like a certain ethnic group – sometimes by orienting more or less to broader local linguistic norms. For example, Hazen (2002) demonstrates that in a tri-ethnic North Carolina community, copula absence rates were predicted by an intersection of ethnic identity and orientation toward the local county versus external areas; Hazen writes, "being an expanded-identity [externally oriented] Native American is different from being a local-identity Native American" (p. 253). More recently, King (2021) examines the retreat from the NCS feature of BAT-retraction amongst African American speakers in Rochester, NY, noting that the orientation toward the particular persona of a mobile Black professional led speakers to avoid the NCS-linked fronted BAT and instead produce more backed BAT realizations – the extralocal norm. Benheim & D'Onofrio (2024) conduct an examination of Jewish Chicagoans, who characterize locally Jewish ways of speaking in terms of New York City English stereotypes – raised THOUGHT in particular – while in actuality employing none of those features in action; instead, they differ from non-Jewish Chicagoans in terms of their level of retreat from the Northern Cities Shift (NCS) – essentially how NON-local they sound.

There is also significant evidence that gender and sexuality are performed in place-specific ways. Podesva (2011) tracks how aspects of the California Vowel Shift (CVS) change in the speech of a gay man who uses more features of the CVS around friends, highlighting a 'gay, partier' persona, and less advanced CVS features in other situations. Here, CVS is not only place-linked but also available to index other characteristics that are also linked to California (e.g., fun, easy-going, etc.) in ways that intersect with specifically LGBT ways of enacting these characteristics. Also in California, Podesva & Van Hofwegen (2014) discuss how ideas about gender norms and 'country orientation' affect productions of /s/ in socially conservative rural towns, wherein retracted /s/ indexes a 'country' orientation; their analysis highlights how LGBT members in this community are able to use this localized, place-linked linguistic resource in ways that express their LGBT identity safely within the speech community norms. In Copenhagen, /s/-variation also intersects in notable ways with gender, sexuality, and locality, as Pharao et al. (2014) demonstrate in work on 'modern' versus 'street' Copenhagen dialects; they argue that fronted /s/ realizations index femininity and gayness more in 'modern' ways of speaking and is not as socially significant when combined with aspects of 'street' language.

Thus, place-linked identity factors do not work in isolation and must be considered alongside (and intersectionally with) other social factors.

3.8 Summary of Place in Sociolinguistics

We have demonstrated that sociolinguistic research has engaged with questions of place identity in a number of ways, without necessarily always participating in a broader conversation about the role of *place* in our analyses. The methods described throughout this section range from qualitative to quantitative, large-scale to micro-studies, production to perception. We advocate for greater awareness about the role of *place* across these varied approaches, and deeper consideration about the conclusions that can be drawn about place from these sociolinguistic studies.

4 Place in Allied Fields

In this section, we aim to provide some context about the interdisciplinary nature of *place*, identifying some of the frameworks, concepts, and tools that sociolinguists can mobilize from allied fields in the humanities and social sciences. We concede that such a brief overview will naturally be superficial. Drawing from fields as diverse as sociology, anthropology, geography, among others with long lineages, enormous literatures, and numerous subdisciplines, in addition to numerous (and sometimes contentious) intra-discipline differences in viewpoints, we cannot nor do we aim for a full picture of these perspectives. Our goal here is to underscore the fact that many disciplines have posed questions centered on *place*, and (socio)linguistics deserves a seat at the table for these discussions.

We have established that place has distinct effects on language, echoing Seale and Mallinson (2018: xiv), who write, "language is affected by material dynamics of migration, residential patterns, the inter-twined development of technology and media, and the everyday context of social exchange in the pursuit of survival." But we would push this statement further to point out that language also affects migration, residence, technology, media, and so on; thus, we encourage greater work at the interface of linguistics and place theory, via engagement with other fields. We each have things to learn from one another. We offer this brief section with some fundamental concepts and representative work on *place* across fields, to provide readers in sociolinguistics with a jumping-off point to begin a much deeper dive into the aspects of place theory that suit their particular projects or goals.

4.1 Defining Place & Space

Across disciplines, researchers have pondered how to both define and delineate *space* and *place*. In his influential work on place in human geography, Yi-Fu Tuan (1977, 1980, 1991) has provided philosophical backing for the humanistic components of place-making. Tuan (1977) exemplifies this conversation, as he considers how humans reconceptualize undifferentiated *space* into meaningful *place,* arguing that it is through sensory experience that a *place* becomes imbued with meaning and is no longer merely *space*. And yet, what exactly happens within that morphing process? Does one arrive upon a conception of a place using emotion, reason, intuition, or some other human faculty entirely? Political geographer Agnew (1987) provides the tripartite characterization seen in Figure 1, in which *place* is defined via three interrelated but somewhat independent aspects – locale, location, and sense of place.

Locale is where daily life and the connections between various entities occur, whereas location denotes the broader social and economic area in which life occurs. One might consider locale as more organic, whereas location is typically defined by larger institutions. Sense of place is the psychosocial and emotional connection that an individual has toward this area.

Yet place does not exist in a vacuum; rather it intersects with many other social constructs in society. In a central volume to the field of geography, Massey (1994) theorizes about the ways that a society's beliefs about gender influence their conceptions of place. She argues that certain places are gendered, and they invite different gendered bodies to inhabit them. She notes that certain places have more (or less) meaning because certain types of people are allowed there, while others are excluded. In this extended conceptualization of place, the locale and location remain constant, but the sense of place shifts. As certain individuals are invited into and/or participate within a space, the sense of place and the connotations of place might change. Addressing the dimension of time, however, Massey clarifies how

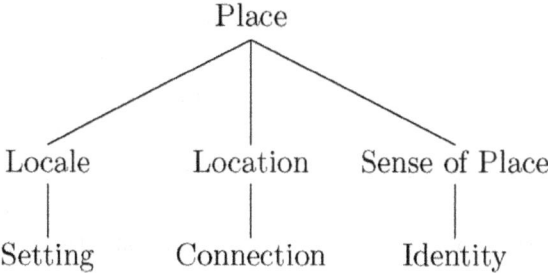

Figure 1 Visualization of Agnew's (1987) tripartite characterization of place (adapted from Reed 2020a).

a place exists in a particular point in space-time, noting that places can and do evolve (and so does their concomitant meaning to members of society). For example, one's physical connection to a particular locale may shift as borders move or as annexation happens, and one's sense of place may change due to large-scale demographic change or as infrastructure developments change the experience of inhabiting that space.

As a social construct, places and spaces feature sometimes arbitrary rules about their location and membership. Anderson (2006) introduces the idea of imagined community. This concept can function at any scale, but Anderson noted how nation-states in particular are truly a (relatively recent) construct that only exist in the minds of its members, and those who acknowledge these imagined borders. Crucially, he states that members of these imagined communities may not actually know many co-members, but may still feel fellowship with them as a part of their (imagined) extended network, due to the shared connection to – and conception of – *place*.

4.2 Place and Placelessness

While places can have member-internal meaning – in the ways that a person may develop deep and personal ties to a place due to their physical and social connection to it – places can also develop meaning via more explicit processes. In particular, we see this reification of places in the tourism industry. The idea of *branding* and commodification of a given place is one that researchers in sociology, anthropology, and geography have considered within the neoliberal landscape of corporatized destinations (cf. Gotham 2007). In these capitalism-driven distillations of what a place is, and how one ought to experience it, the outsider perspective is placed front & center, and authenticity and nuance can take a backseat to a more curated presentation of a place. In the process, some writers note, the 'Disneyfication' of place can occur, in which a narrow and idealized version of that locale is presented to outsiders (Eeckhout 2001; Souther 2007). This process inherently decenters and marginalizes 'undesirable' inhabitants or features. Thus we see how place-as-commodified-good can impact who gets to make an authentic claim to what 'counts' as that place's identity, members, and other qualities.

Alongside this reified conception of place comes its converse: *placelessness,* or the idea of the *non-place*. Most deeply theorized by Relph (1976), Kunstler (1993), and Arefi (1999), the idea of placelessness in modern society is one accompanied by equal parts angst and nostalgia. While Arefi and Kunstler focus their analyses on placelessness as a form of loss in the face of the systematic destruction of a place's distinctiveness, Relph notes in particular the anxiety of modern society about the ways that the pressures of modern life have eradicated our personal connections to the place in our everyday experiences. This eradication creates an epidemic of inauthenticity with respect to places, as this lack of differentiation raises a sense of unease and disconnect in its inhabitants. These 'placeless' places – he identifies the example of strip malls and suburban subdivisions – cease to be unique, and might be seen as commodified, uniform, or consolidated.

Some scholars (e.g., the volume by McClay & McAllister 2014 and entries therein) point out that 'placelessness' can derive from our reliance on technology, in particular how we utilize tools such as GPS or location-based apps. In using these modern tools, we offload much of the effort in learning the nuances of a place (such as finding one's way or where to get the best meal), and we do not fully engage in where we are. Rather than using suggestions from neighbors or community members or our own experiences, we rely on suggestions from algorithms and online reviews. In doing so, we have the potential to miss, or perhaps to lose, the unique aspects of each place (Shulman 2014). This loss can make each place seem more uniform, as we have not fully experienced each place; rather, we are relying on what others say, or what an algorithm generates from what others have said, about a place. By only experiencing a purposely narrowed version of place, any vestige of what makes a place unique – from quaint neighborhood spaces to local dialectal features – is missed as visitors experience only a small, curated portion of a locale, or they travel routes dictated by shortest time or fewest tolls.

Beyond the 'disembodied' question of technological mediation of places, the modern person's lack of connection to a given place may also be attributed to political decisions about transportation, roadways, and other policy ideas about transportation infrastructure (Kunstler 1993). Many of these decisions have been made over the past century with certain goals in mind – traffic reduction, maintenance of speed of travel, and connection of population centers. However, some of these decisions have actually made congestion worse because highways permitted more sprawl and the need for more traffic (Toth 2014). And as a result, cities have spread out from the urban core, leading many inhabitants to spend enormous amounts of time in transit, not experiencing their hometown beyond what they see through a windshield. Urban neighborhoods and communities tend to be denigrated (think of the phrase 'Inner City' and the dog whistle this phrase represented in the United States in the 1990s), and many of these most disenfranchised residents' homes have historically been destroyed to make way for roadways (with usually racial patterning to these targeted neighborhood razings). Such changes create suburbs – also racially organized – that are oriented around convenience and highways, which discourage residents from building the kind of person-to-person localized connections that create and maintain locally specific ways of speaking.

Another way a place's distinctiveness can be lost is via gentrification, a topic that has been central to many recent sociological studies of urban spaces. Gentrification is an inherently raced and classed phenomenon whereby the character and population of a given neighborhood – most recently observed in the urban core of many major cities, as pushback against suburbification has occurred – change rapidly as a result of an influx of retail and affluent property seekers. Longstanding residents are generally priced out of these neighborhoods as gentrification advances, thereby changing the inherent identity of the place, as well as the locus for the cultural and linguistic practices that had previously been tied to that place.

While displacement can be a result of gentrification, we are also seeing a rise in worldwide displacement due to war, political persecution, and climate crises. Carter, Donald, & Squires (1993: vii) write:

> For many people, displaced and exiled from their homelands, places have long since ceased to provide straight-forward support to their identity. Yet, though the 'homes' which ground and house identities can be denied people physically by enforced exile or lost through chosen migration, they still continue to resonate throughout the imaginations of displaced communities.

When one's physical connection to a place is ruptured by time or space, one may experience grief or loss (Fried 1963). Brown & Perkins (1992) state that furthermore, disruptions in place attachments threaten one's self-definition, decentering the individuals experiencing the rupture and unrooting them from their lens on the world. Longing for home has been shown to be intimately linked to one's rootedness level (McAndrew 1998; Lewicka 2008), and rootedness has in turn been linked to linguistic practices (Reed 2018a, 2020a, 2020b). The timescale component is essential to the idea of rootedness in multiple ways: to begin with, rootedness is defined by being in a place – *staying* in a place – for a long time. Tuan (1980: 3–4) refines this definition by calling rootedness a combination of long-term habitation in, and "a feeling for and attachment to place." He notes that rootedness is typically viewed as "'harmonious stability' rather than 'dynamic progress'" (p. 3). And progress, or change, necessarily implicates the passage of time. A place is always situated in a specific time, as Carmichael & Dajko (2016) note in their employment of Bakhtin's (1981: 84) notion of a *chronotope*, or the "intrinsic connectedness of temporal and spatial relationships" to examine place nostalgia in New Orleans. Indeed, the opposite is true as well: just as nostalgia represents a longing for a given time, that time is always linked to a place. Thus, homesickness is not just the longing to be back in a place, but to be back in our memory of that place. Environmental psychologists Proshansky, Fabian, & Kaminoff (1983: 62) argue that memory is essential to how we define a place, writing:

> The cognitive processes involved in the development of place-identity are not any different from those underlying the formation of other cognitive structures. For example, memories of spaces and places, no less than our memories of social situations, tend to be thematic and stylized.

That is, we define places through memories, which are inherently personal, however, they are sculpted by the existing schemata and ideologies that we are exposed to, similar to the *attitudinal cognitorium* outlined by Preston (2010).

In examining the forces inherent in what Appadurai (1990) terms 'deterritorialization' – which simultaneously captures displacement, migration, and globalization – Appadurai suggests that as we see an increase in physical and geographic detachment of cultural elements tied to a given place (foods, traditions, music, language practices, etc.), we set the stage for commoditization of these artifacts as they become highlighted in their new locale; but we also set the stage for homogenization as a result of these globalizing and intermingling cultures, which by their very nature 'indigenize' quickly as they become embedded in their new homes.

4.3 Place as Sacred

Place has a central focus in myriad religious and faith traditions. Thus, one schemata for examining human relationships with place is via focus on the role of place in these belief systems. Bruggeman (2002: 116–117) writes, "place is space in which vows have been exchanged, promises have been made, and demands have been issued." That is, many spaces have become imbued with a sacred meaning, affecting individual relationships to these places as well as beliefs about what kinds of activities can and should take place in these locales.

The sacred nature of *place* can heighten and/or concentrate the sense of place, but this sense of place might also be contested as the same locale is connected to multiple histories and traditions. Different groups may consider the same place to be sacred in different ways to different faith traditions, or a place may be sacred to one group but not to another; either circumstance, of course, can result in impactful repercussions that resonate beyond one's individual belief system. One key example of a contested sacred site is the Temple Mount in Jerusalem, a place considered holy by three Abrahamic faiths (Judaism, Islam, and Christianity). Each faith lays claim to the precise location and derives portions of their mythology from it. The conflict about whose sacred claim on the land should take precedent has been the source of centuries of tension in Jerusalem. In the built environment, we see similar conflicts play out; for example, many urban spaces have buildings that once housed places of worship that have changed hands. As participation levels waned, these buildings have been sold – to developers, to municipalities, and sometimes to congregations of other faith traditions (Simons, DeWine, & Ledebur 2017). Once the location has been sold, some maintain a connection with what the building once housed (e.g., retaining some aspect of the name), while others do not wish to keep the connection.

Power shifts and the flow of time can also define how sacredness is respected, and we can see this clearly in the case of indigenous sacred spaces colonized by Western powers. An example in the United States is Mount Rushmore, a mountain located in South Dakota carved with likenesses of American presidents on the mountainside. The mountain was considered sacred by the Lakota, the Cheyenne, and the Arapahoe, among other Native American nations, and it was taken from them in the nineteenth century, and then was carved in the early twentieth century. The Supreme Court of the United States ruled in 1980 that the United States had improperly taken the land from the Lakota (McKeever 2020), yet the mountain remains a place where tourists flock (and protesters stage). Similarly, the volcano Mauna Kea in Hawai'i has been the site of intense protest by indigenous groups battling construction of the Thirty Meter Telescope on a sacred site for native Hawai'ians (Miner Murray 2019). This struggle has played out as a microcosm of the colonization efforts of the United States on the Hawai'ian islands, with Western ideas about science, progress, and land ownership prevailing over native attempts to enforce their land sovereignty. An example in which resolution resulted in the acknowledgment of the sacred power of place in indigenous culture comes from Alaska, where in 2015 the largest peak in the state was renamed from Mt. McKinley to the indigenous name Denali. In her speech sharing this news, US Secretary of the Interior Sally Jewell stated:

> This name change recognizes the sacred status of Denali to many Alaska Natives. The name Denali has been official for use by the State of Alaska since 1975, but even more importantly, the mountain has been known as Denali for generations. With our own sense of reverence for this place, we are officially renaming the mountain Denali in recognition of the traditions of Alaska Natives and the strong support of the people of Alaska. (US Department of the Interior 2015)

This battle over *linguistic* sovereignty, or the right name places, plays out in other colonized locales such as New Zealand, where the Māori party has called to change the country's name back to the Māori language name of Aotearoa, with little acknowledgment from other political leaders in the country (Chang, Intagliata, & Handel 2022).

The sacred nature of places adds an additional dimension to the sense of place, as what this place means may be inextricably linked to who a person considers themselves to be, given that religion is a crucial part of an individual's identity. Furthermore, how that sacred place connects to broader systems and outside entities can and does impact the location. Returning to our former houses of worship example, once the building is sold, how does it connect to the community? Certain individuals may view it as where they were married or where they worshipped, while others may view it now as a chance for affordable housing or a new coffee shop. The inherent contradiction and tension between these two views aptly demonstrate how central *place* and its connections and meanings can be.

4.4 Mobilizing Concepts from Allied Fields

Throughout this Element, we have identified examples of what allied fields view as the salient and worthy-of-study aspects of *place*. Sociolinguists may benefit from considering these varied frameworks and viewpoints as we think about how to define and study place in our own work. In this section, we offer some direction about how this might be accomplished, while also establishing some areas where we believe sociolinguists can contribute to inquiries about *place*, which on the whole are lacking a linguistic lens.

We begin by identifying the range of place-related terms from different fields and how they are frequently used, noting that as these terms cross-pollinate between fields they may change in meaning or association. In a number of papers across disciplines, researchers will include more than one of these terms, a nod to the challenge of finding a shared lexicon across fields with an interest in *place* (see Patterson & Williams 2005 on the challenges inherent in seeking a coherent cross-discipline theorization of *place*).

Though many of these terms significantly overlap – compare place identity and sense of place, for example, or place attachment and place orientation – we wish to also draw attention to how different subfields theorize about *place* for specific purposes that relate to the questions of interest for that field. For example, it is perhaps unsurprising that sociology and environmental psychology are centered on aspects of identity, emotion, attitude, and memory – cognitive and behavioral components of how humans orient to *place*. Or in design fields such as architecture and landscape architecture we see researchers point to the notably visual, aesthetic aspects of *place*. While we in sociolinguistics have our own specific purposes in research that have also shaped how we approach *place* (mostly centering on this factor as an explanatory, demographic quality of participants), the authors of this Element emphasize that these different approaches from allied fields are also capturing something very real about how humans relate to *place*, and it may prove generative (or at the very least informative) to borrow and/or consider these lenses in our research on sociolinguistic patterns.

Table 2 Place terms and their meanings/applications across fields

Term	Meaning/application	Field/citation
Place identity	The social and affective connections individuals have to places (especially home); sometimes described as a "sub-structure of self-identity" (Proshansky, Fabian, & Kaminoff 1983: 59)	Psychology, especially social psychology and environmental psychology (Proshansky, Fabian, & Kaminoff 1983)
Place-based identity	Used similarly to place identity; the bonds individuals have with their homes, that over time become embedded in their personal sense of identity	Tourism (Wang, Chen, & Xu 2019), communication (Walker 2007)
Place attachment	The physical, behavioral, and emotional embeddedness that humans have in places; their feelings of connectedness to a place, and behaviors that enact this connection. Often measured specifically via surveys and demographic information such as length of dwelling in a place; connections to neighbors; etc.)	Sociology, social psychology (Low & Altman 2012), and geography (Diener & Hagen 2021)
Place orientation	The dynamic connections individuals may have to places where they live, work, or interact. Castle, Wu, & Weber (2011: 192) define this as "an integrated set of attitudes, beliefs, and predispositions that the person holds toward places, including rural and urban places."	Sociology (Miller & Rivera 2010), economics (Castle, Wu, & Weber 2011)

Sense of place/*genius loci*	Generally treated as the intangible character of a place; the elements that altogether make up that place's identity	Architecture (Norberg-Schulz 1980), geography (Tuan 1991; Cresswell 2015)
Place-making; place-shaping	Generally viewed as the active behaviors that create either the physical location or the experience of moving through that location (usually design-oriented, but sometimes extended metaphorically to mean the community behaviors that create a place identity or shared sense of place)	Architecture (Arefi 2013), landscape architecture (Stilgenbauer 2015)
Landscape	Primarily considered in visual terms, often with regard to its aesthetic appeal	Architecture, landscape architecture, art

We wish to draw particular attention to the ways certain fields seek to capture and study the ways we consume *place* (as an experience) and store it (as a memory); that is, how we process *place* as an embodied sensory experience. Researchers and practitioners in design fields dedicate rigorous and systematic attention toward identifying what makes a place beautiful – how do humans respond to the sensory experience of that place, not limited only to the visual plane but the full range of one's experience moving through that space? This experience, crucially, can evoke a very specific 'sense of place' that is more than a strict sum of its parts; it can include, for example, subjective reactions to a given place, associations between known places, and memories of past places. Within the design world, form and function go hand in hand when considering how individuals form attachments to certain places. For example, in a study of the Kuala Lumpur city centre in Malaysia, Ujang (2012) asked shopkeepers and shoppers in three shopping areas about their emotional versus functional attachment to these locales, considering how these factors were affected by typical activities completed in the area, physical elements in the space, and viewpoints on the 'image' of the centre (e.g., charm; uniqueness; safety). This marriage of the aesthetic – the visual plane – and the practical – focusing on functionality and use – is central to the idea of place-making. Rarely if ever are the aesthetic qualities of place considered in any linguistic work, despite the fact that humans clearly orient to aesthetic components of *place*. The design world has also crucially noted how a *lack* of some aesthetic quality might be associated with a place (e.g., urban blight, aftermath of strip mining, inter alia). This lack or loss of 'beauty' might then be associated with the people who live or are from this place, and come to be associated with their other qualities – such as their linguistic practices. Research on tourism, language commodification, and linguistic landscape perhaps comes closest to capturing these aspects of place aesthetic, though we would encourage broader engagement with this idea.

In addition, research in fields like human geography and landscape architecture have broached the question of what makes a place feel less distinctive, less 'like itself,' as a Geography of Nowhere (Kunstler 1993) has taken hold of many man-made landscapes, in the United States and elsewhere. These processes take place via standardization and globalization, resulting in housing structures and retail options becoming less locally distinctive, and crucially less suited to the specific ecosystem in which they are situated. So, too, have conversations in linguistics veered toward questions of global language trends, shifts away from historically local ways of speaking, and the linguistic effect of our greater connectedness thanks to the speed and ubiquity of online communication. We suggest these threads might be united, and might benefit from engagement with one another, as we consider language practices to be yet another vehicle of social and cultural change.

The question of placelessness is not frequently considered through a linguistic lens, although arguably any work on dialect leveling and standardization is in a way about a dialect becoming untethered from place. Agha (2003) in his description of enregisterment – a concept that has been essential to theorizing about the processes that lead to connections between language and place – notes that in particular, Received Pronunciation, or the enregistered standardized British accent, "is a supra-local accent; it is enregistered in public awareness as indexical of speaker's class and level of education; it is valued precisely for effacing the geographic origins of speaker" (233). In their examination of the New Town of Milton Keynes in England, Kerswill & Williams (2000) delve deeply into the question of migration across space and individual connections to prior hometowns, but interestingly do not place a lens on the evolving identity of Milton Keynes as a (non-place). Milton Keynes is an interesting example, as it was a planned city – chosen and situated as to be equidistant from several urban centers. Notably, thus, it was not a place that was sacred, nor did it have a long history. In fact, it had *no history*, and no personal connection for individuals who lived there. Rather, as a planned settlement to relieve housing congestion in London, Milton Keynes was a city with a utilitarian purpose (nota bene: in contrast to other 'new towns,' Milton Keynes was accessible with developed public transportation and a modernist architecture [Clapson 2013]). There is interest in considering what it means as the speakers develop an emplaced dialect in a 'non-place,' such as this.

Part of the reason that 'placeless places' are such an uncomfortable notion for humans is because of the personal connections to places that we seek out. When considering Agnew's three aspects of place – locale, location, and sense of place – it is crucial to note that there is an increasing scale of subjectivity in terms of both personal relationships and specific meanings associated with a place. That is: place is personal, and the experience of places is subjective, by definition. In variationist sociolinguistics, there is a history of examining language patterns in the aggregate, considering the effects of broader social factors on variation, with many discussions centering on how to rigorously operationalize identity factors and stances. We suggest that acknowledgment of the subjectivity of place attachment and place identity need not result in a lack of rigor. Just as the field has gamely broached increasingly nuanced questions of personal identities and stances related to gender, sexuality, and ethnicity without sacrificing systematicity and potential for generalizability, so too might we acknowledge the varied, changing, and personal relationships participants may have with the places they spend time over the course of their lives.

Place as memory provides another useful lens for consideration. While indeed some aspects of one's sense of place might be shared, especially when the memory is part of local (or national) discussion and dialogue, idiosyncrasies may also be present, as not all memories are shared or logged in the same way. Moreover, as a place changes – because all places are in flux – this meaning may not even be available to others. Thus, the particular meaning of a place for an individual might now only live in their memory. For example, Paul (the second author) has distinct memories of working on a parcel of land as an adolescent. However, that land has now passed hands and a particular barn no longer exists. That place now only exists in memories; many of those memories are only Paul's. In work on memory and nostalgia in environmental psychology, researchers argue that indeed our relationships with places have cognitive consequences in how we store and remember places. Lewicka (2008) conducted a study of how residents of Lviv, Ukraine and Wrocław, Poland described their memories of these cities, which in the past were part of a single country, though borders were redrawn following World War II. Via surveys and interviews, Lewicka demonstrated that place attachment was predictive of how residents remembered and discussed their respective cities. Furthermore, residents had differing scales of orientation – in Lviv, orientation tended to be on the national scale, while in Wrocław the memory of the place was primarily on a local scale. Thus our memories of places can be affected by both top-down factors – such as border-redrawing and national mythologies – and bottom-up factors – more individualized and localized memories of places.

The idea of *place* as sacred, as homeland, is almost so obvious to us as humans to be unworthy of mention, and yet this visceral connection to *place* is often treated as outside of the scope of linguistic research. We can indeed, though, interrogate just what makes one feel so connected to a place. Paradoxically, as we have described earlier at various points – both longstanding rootedness in place, and distancing or removal from a place, can equally exert force upon one's sense of connectedness to one's homeplace. We see both sides of this, for example, in the question of indigenous claims to ancestral lands alongside language revitalization movements. We can also see it in research on diaspora – movement across space by individuals who share a common homeland; and indeed, although diaspora is often considered in terms of culture, ethnicity, religion, or other uniting bonds, the definition itself centers on place. We think linguists have much to learn about the sacredness of *place* by more deeply engaging with these ideas of connectedness and claim to place, rather than treating such subjectivities as outside the purview of our research.

Any discussion of place must also include thoughts related to access – who gets to be in a place, who gets ascribed as belonging, or who gets welcomed into a place. Here, place intersects with numerous other factors and features – gender, ethnicity, race, class, age, and ideologies related to perceptions of one's in-group versus out-group status. Many places have disputed, contradictory, or disparate meanings because not everyone has access or is allowed to be in a space. We might think here about certain neighborhoods within a city or the well-known view of which 'side of the tracks' someone lives or is from. Or, perhaps, certain groups were there, but they do not exist in the connotation of that place in the popular mind, (cf. Cresswell 2015 for discussions of the erasure of homeless, transgender, and other marginalized identities from certain spaces). Consider Appalachia, a place that typically evokes notions of whiteness. However, persons of color have always existed within Appalachia – hence the thriving and growing recognition of *Affrilachia* and Affrilachians (e.g., Walker 2000). And yet, non-white folks were not discussed during the myth-making process because of circulating prejudices and thus are not always part of the popular conception of the region. Such an example connects the two types of meaning – denotational and connotational. Appalachia denotes a region, but it connotes for many a white region, which is decidedly an incomplete conceptualization.

Such considerations about inclusion and exclusion apply equally to researcher decisions – both in terms of decisions about who to *include in and exclude from* studies (cf. Bucholtz 2003 on authenticity and participant selection) and about what defines a given place – which can of course be impacted by researchers' own conceptions of *place* (cf. Britain 2017 on the 'urban/rural gaze' in dialectology). Identifying a place as the site of research also brings in questions of scale. In sociolinguistics, we have indeed considered varied scales of community, ranging from microcommunities (e.g., communities of practice [Eckert & McConnell-Ginet 1992; Mallinson & Childs 2007] and even individual speakers [Rickford & McNair-Knox 1994; Podesva 2007]) to global movements (e.g., uptalk as a phenomenon in various world Englishes [Warren 2016] and the globalization of hip-hop [Pennycook 2007]). While many studies on language and place center on the city/regional/national affiliation level – for example, in New Orleans (Schoux Casey 2013; Carmichael 2017, 2023), in Appalachia (Reed 2016, 2020a), amongst relocated Canadians in NYC (Nycz 2018, 2019), in the Asturias (Barnes 2016) and Andalusia (Villena-Ponsoda & Vida-Castro 2020) regions in Spain, and in rural Maine (Pabst 2022) – yet others examine neighborhood-level affiliation, for example, Becker (2014) in New York City, D'Onofrio and Benheim (2019) in Chicago, Sneller (2019) in Philadelphia, and Baranowski (2023) in Manchester. And indeed, a single individual may have allegiances to multiple levels of scale, and differing definitions about the key boundaries of a place – both worthy of probing further in our work. Oppositions at varied levels – urban versus rural, suburb versus city, center versus periphery – have been central to conceptions of *place* in sociology, human geography, and other allied fields, and it is worthwhile to seek out and mobilize their theoretical tools for making sense of these categories, and the stances that individuals take toward them. What is meaningful to a speaker may be meaningfully reflected in their speech, and we risk missing that by failing to investigate such questions in our methods and analysis.

While the preceding sections may read as a guidebook for plundering other fields' tools, we also wish to point out what is saliently missing from interdisciplinary work on *place* up to now: a linguistic lens. Indeed, in our examination of *place* in allied fields we noted many cases of cross-pollination between varied fields with a stake in defining how humans conceive of and engage with place; notably none of these fields cite or read sociolinguistic work on language and place. And yet language is at the heart of how we describe and engage with *place*, as humans, and can also be a way of expressing our link with our homeplace – via the language practices indexically tied to that place (be that on the level of a language, dialect, ways of interacting, or so on). Language can also be a tool for demonstrating how humans remain connected across space, and even in disembodied places like the Internet. When thinking about sense of place, and the distinct *sensory* components of that, we must acknowledge that soundscape – the voices of people from a place – is the one of the most evocative aspects of a locale. Just as making use of tools from allied fields can improve our work, by engaging with their research, we can also pull these fields into conversation with us, so that they might see the value in making use of linguistic analysis tools in their own research on *place*.

In Sections 5 and 6, we provide two case studies merging sociolinguistic methods and interdisciplinary approaches to *place*, via examinations of (sub) urban New Orleans and rural Appalachia. Crucially, we seek to demonstrate examples of the contributions that place theory can make to understanding emplaced sociolinguistic variation. We argue that without this lens, we cannot understand the ways that speakers' experiences with these places – and their ideologies about people from other places – play a critical role in their linguistic choices. In Section 7, we draw together these disparate threads noting the role of *place* in each case, and illustrating the varied ways that we have mobilized aspects of the previously described place theory contributions.

5 The View from the Periphery: Agency, Authenticity, and Place Orientation in Post-Katrina Greater New Orleans

5.1 Introduction

Sociolinguists have often considered the role of center-periphery relationships – for example in terms of spread and diffusion of change in dialect geography (cf. Auer 2010), and via research theorizing social networks of speakers (e.g., Milroy &

Milroy 1978). More recently researchers have further probed the implications of intersecting forms of peripheralization – geographic and social – and the ways that the social meaning of these forms of marginalization may be in conflict or build upon each other. For example, in the introduction to their edited volume on language and place-making in peripheral spaces, Cornips & DeRooij (2018: 3) write, "[t]o understand the power dimension in processes of centralization-peripheralization, one needs to address the question of how social-economic, and political and spatial understandings of the periphery […] give rise to (feelings of) linguistic marginalization." Several researchers consider this question in terms of suburbification, especially within the US context. Silverstein (2014) for example points to the exurbs of New York City as the current home of enregistered (Agha 2003) NYC linguistic features, rather than the core neighborhoods of Manhattan where they took root, noting a disconnect between the perceived authenticity of the center city versus the true locus of 'authentic' NYC accents. In his analysis of the diffusion of linguistic change in St. Louis, Missouri suburbs, Duncan (2019) dedicates significant space to discussing the development of American suburbs and the way history has shaped these communities and their inhabitants – that is, how the geographic and linguistic are inseparably intertwined. In the analysis that follows, I draw on this line of research to examine how linguistic features found in the periphery can index various place-based identities – and other related indexical qualities – depending on the context and user within post-Katrina Greater New Orleans.

In Greater New Orleans, the traditional white, working class dialect of English – often called 'Yat' – sounds similar to New York City English, making it stand out within the linguistic landscape of the American South. This variety is frequently performed in media and interaction to index localness and authenticity, and long-term ties to the city (Coles 2001); such markers are especially valued following the destruction and upheaval of Hurricane Katrina in 2005 (Carmichael & Dajko 2016; Dajko & Carmichael 2023). Though historically indexical of the working class New Orleanians who spoke this way, this variety has developed a third-order indexicality (Silverstein 2003) tying it to New Orleans as a place (Mucciaccio 2009; Schoux Casey 2013), in a similar process as took place in Pittsburgh over time (Johnstone, Andrus, & Danielson 2006). Crucially, though, in New Orleans, these features "moved to the suburbs" a generation ago, and are most commonly heard now – non-performatively – now in the suburb of Chalmette, the residents of which are playfully (and sometimes derogatively) called Chalmatians. In prior work (Carmichael 2017, 2023), I have demonstrated that, amongst Chalmatians, these local 'Yat' features are used at higher rates amongst those most oriented toward Chalmette, as opposed to external places. In the analysis that follows, I argue that this continued use of stigmatized features is an agentive act which indirectly indexes a Chalmette insider stance, one that rejects external understandings of Chalmette as a place, as well as its social, spatial, and linguistic peripheralization by New-Orleans-centered locals.

5.2 Language, Space, and Place in Greater New Orleans

Located just before the terminus of the Mississippi River into the Gulf of Mexico, New Orleans has historically represented a crucial site for the import and export of goods. As a result, throughout its history, this territory frequently changed hands between French, Spanish, and English rule. In 1803, the United States doubled its size by purchasing the Louisiana territory from Napoleon, however, it was not until after the Civil War that New Orleans became a primarily Anglophone city (Brasseaux 2005). Irish immigrants fleeing the potato famine arrived en masse throughout the 1800s, followed by waves of immigrants from Sicily and Germany (Campanella 2006). These immigrants often found employment in the fishing and shipping industry of this port city, settling in certain areas of the city where commingling and intermarriage between French, German, Italian, and Irish residents of New Orleans was common (Dillard 1985). These immigrant groups were often defined by the space they occupied, such as the working-class neighborhoods of the Irish Channel and the Ninth Ward, where a distinct dialect of English developed. The label 'Yat' came to be applied to both the residents and their way of speaking. This term comes from the common greeting "where y'at?" (Eble 2006). The Yat dialect has arguably been enregistered (Agha 2003) since the 1980s (cf. Kolker & Alvarez 1985) as 'THE' local New Orleans accent with "symbolic value as part of 'authentic' New Orleans" (Coles 2001: 74). Linguistic features associated with this dialect include phonological features such as variable nonrhoticity, raised THOUGHT, and a split short-a system, as well as certain syntactic constructions and a number of distinctive lexical items (see Mucciaccio 2009 or Carmichael 2014 for an exhaustive list).

As happened in a number of US cities, the latter half of the twentieth century brought a significant wave of suburban expansion into surrounding areas (no small feat in New Orleans, where in many cases this required backfill of swamps and marshes, and engineering of flood prevention measures). Racial integration of schools took place in the middle of the twentieth century, and was, as in many other Southern locales, a time of violence and bigotry in the city as a whole, the wounds of which remain clearly apparent to this day. At this time, many white residents of Orleans Parish relocated to the suburban outlying areas across parish lines, where de facto school segregation took place, via residential segregation. Chalmette, located just over the parish line from the Lower Ninth Ward neighborhood of New Orleans, and the site of a number of factories and oil refineries along the Mississippi River, became home to a significant amount of white, working-class Yat speakers, and over time came to be known within

Language and Place

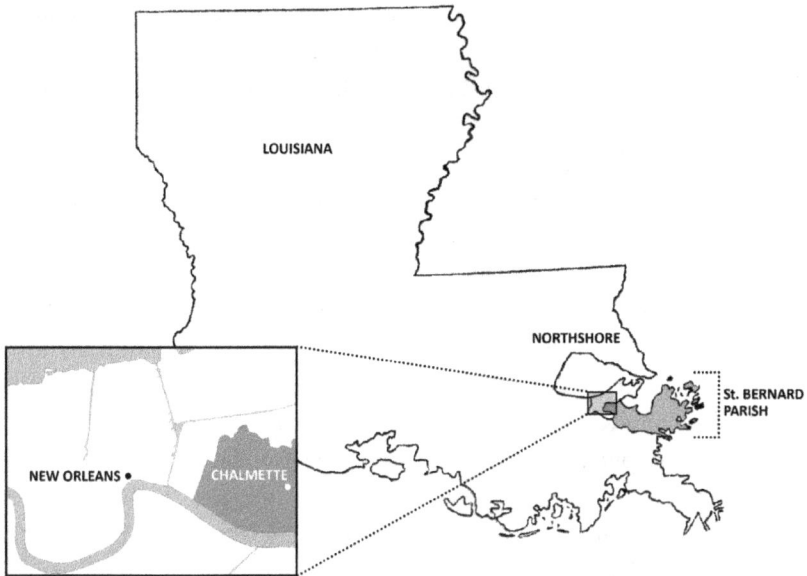

Figure 2 Chalmette and the Northshore in relation to New Orleans, Louisiana.

Greater New Orleans as being the locus of the Yat dialect (Robley 1994; Mucciaccio 2009; Carmichael 2014). Figure 2 demonstrates the location of Chalmette, within St. Bernard Parish, in relation to New Orleans.

Mucciaccio (2009) has theorized that the enregisterment of Yat started with the white, working class residents of the Lower Ninth Ward, and eventually spread to encapsulate all white, working class residents within Greater New Orleans, including Chalmatians (many of whom descended from the original Lower Ninth Ward Yats). Thus, over time, the social and linguistic stereotypes centered on Yats have shifted spatially, to center on the suburban town of Chalmette. The features used by Yats, however, have also developed a third-order indexicality tying them to New Orleans authenticity in general. As Schoux Casey (2013: 148) writes, "Yat is now predominantly a suburban dialect, even though mediated activity frequently promotes it as *the* New Orleans dialect" (emphasis in original).

Greater New Orleans has seen drastic social and political changes over the past decade, primarily due to the aftermath of Hurricane Katrina. Hurricane Katrina made landfall in Louisiana on August 29, 2005, flooding 80 percent of the city and leaving a wave of chaos in its wake due to the slow federal emergency response. The hurricane's destruction left many residents homeless, leading large proportions of the population to permanently relocate from their previous homes to areas unaffected by the storm, in Louisiana or further. The low-lying suburban town of Chalmette, located just downriver from New Orleans, was particularly hard-hit. In addition to flooding due to the storm surge, Chalmette was also the site of the largest residential oil spill after Katrina, when a ruptured tank released over 1 million gallons of crude oil into the floodwaters, making many homes already damaged by flooding also dangerously unlivable due to the oil. High numbers of Chalmette residents permanently relocated after Katrina, with over half of these individuals leaving for other areas of Greater New Orleans at higher elevations or with more effective flood prevention measures (Lasley 2012), diffusing this enclave community and bringing them into increased contact with other residents around the city.

The storm also brought a wave of newcomers into New Orleans, who have gentrified historic neighborhoods near the city center, pricing out many long-standing locals who returned to rebuild after the storm (Dajko & Carmichael 2023). These post-Katrina changes in the city have brought with them the battle for New Orleans authenticity (playfully described in online spaces as the fight to be 'Nolier than thou'), as newcomers and locals, cityfolk and suburbanites, returners and relocators have grappled with defining what it means to embody a New Orleans identity.

5.3 Methods and Analysis

The insights presented in this analysis come from three main sources: (1) ethnographic observations around Greater New Orleans and interviews with fifty-seven Chalmatians, some of whom permanently relocated from Chalmette after the storm (sample described in detail in Carmichael 2014); (2) memes and social media posts; and (3) artifacts and commodified goods sold in and around the city of New Orleans. I thus analyze participants' discourse about Chalmette and other parts of Greater New Orleans in tandem with widely circulating ideologies about place, via memes and commodified goods in the city. In doing so, I am able to situate linguistic moves being made by participants in my sample within the broader sociolinguistic landscape of post-Katrina New Orleans, and the shifting ideologies of language and place in this post-disaster context.

All participants are referred to by self-chosen pseudonyms, and identified with basic sociodemographic information: their birth year, gender identity (self-identified), and their simplified extra-Chalmatian orientation score, binned for simplicity here into three categories: very Chalmette-oriented (−5 to 0); somewhat externally oriented (1–5); and very externally oriented (>5). The calculation of extra-Chalmatian orientation scores is described in detail in Carmichael (2023), and raw scores are provided in Online Appendix along with other detailed demographic information about each participant.

5.4 Chalmette on the Periphery: Social, Spatial, and Linguistic Marginalization

Central to the geography of New Orleans are the many waterways that surround and cut through the city – canals, bayous, marshes, a river, a lake, and the Gulf of Mexico. In no area of New Orleans is the divisive power of water clearer than in the Eastern portion of the city, in New Orleans East and the Lower Ninth Ward out to St. Bernard Parish. These parts of the city are accessible from the rest of New Orleans only by bridge, following the construction of the Industrial Canal in the 1920s, which connects the Mississippi River to Lake Pontchartrain and effectively cuts off the land to the East of the canal (Campanella 2010). There are only three roads that lead to Chalmette from outside St. Bernard Parish: two from the Ninth Ward, and one that crosses four miles of marshland by way of a large suspended steel bridge connecting St. Bernard to New Orleans East; Figure 3 demonstrates these three roads.

This geographic isolation is viewed as an asset to residents, as Big G and Parrain explain:

> Big G (b. 1962, male, very Chalmette-oriented): "The only way you can get to St. Bernard is if you get off the interstate path and go towards the south, in the corner. Now, nobody would go to that corner unless they have a reason to. So you don't get all this influence from the rest of the world. From–from–you don't get all this influence like from uh [the western middle class suburb of] Metairie, and New Orleans, and North – you know. It's our own little world."[2]

> Parrain (b. 1969, male, very Chalmette-oriented): "Unless you need to come here [Chalmette] for something specifically, to visit someone or get something specifically, or to go fishing or hunting, there's no reason to come through here. So we don't get no–no–no traffic come through here."[3]

Big G identifies 'influence' as being limited – and indeed, this lack of external 'influence' or exposure is likely the reason that Chalmette residents retained many of the linguistic features that speakers in other parts of Greater New Orleans shifted away from a generation earlier. The geographic isolation of Chalmette has also caused social isolation, resulting in an incredibly insular community, in which dense, multiplex networks and strong intergenerational ties are common.

> Justin (b. 1982, male, very Chalmette-oriented): "everybody's so close down there, it's like one big family – everybody knows everybody, I mean you can go to the store and you're gonna see somebody you know or you go out to eat down there you're gonna see somebody you know, you know everybody down there."[4]

---
[2] Accompanying audio file Sound 1 is available at www.cambridge.org/EISO_Carmichael
[3] Accompanying audio file Sound 2 is available at www.cambridge.org/EISO_Carmichael
[4] Accompanying audio file Sound 3 is available at www.cambridge.org/EISO_Carmichael

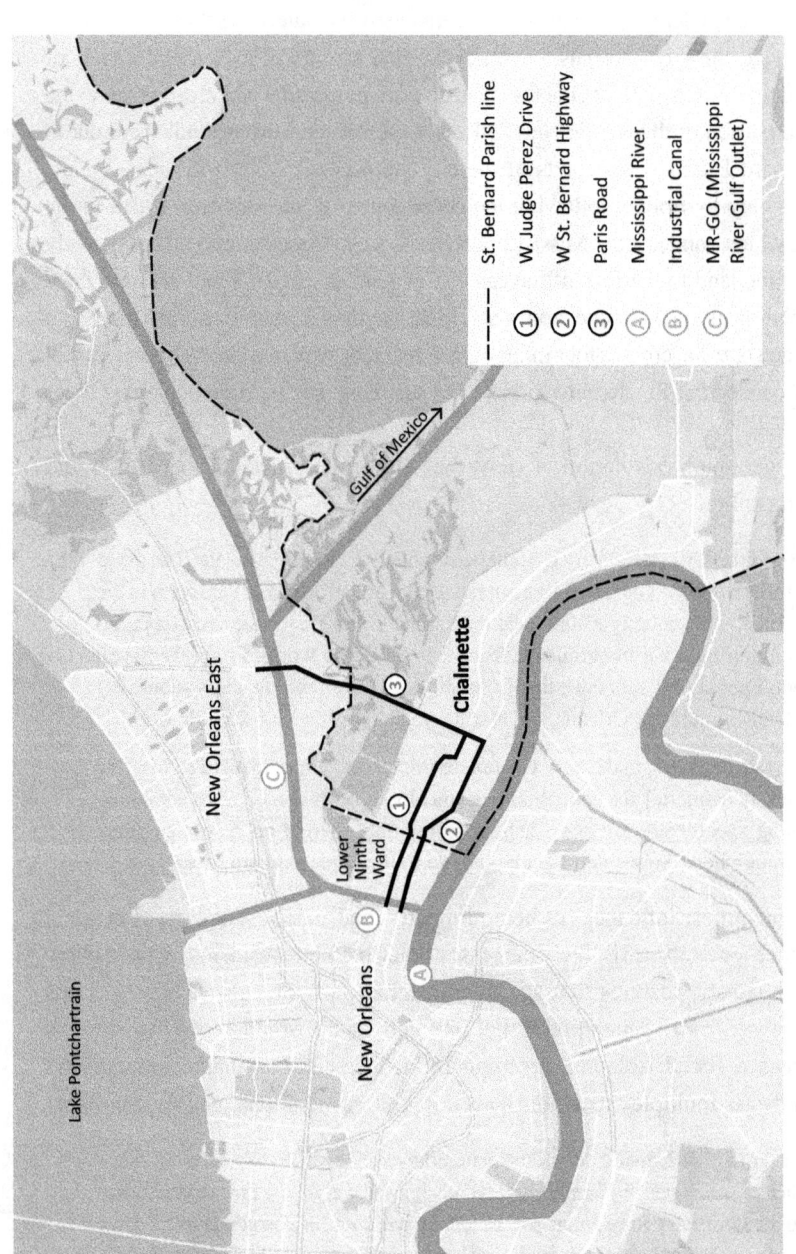

Figure 3 Roads into (and out of) Chalmette.

> Benjamin (b. 1981, male, somewhat externally-oriented): "You don't find a lot of people who just come from outside of St. Bernard to move into St. Bernard. It's a lot of second, third, fourth generation families that are born and raised there, they have their kids there, they live, you know, a few houses down from each other."[5]

Some went so far as to describe Chalmette – and St. Bernard Parish more broadly – as a "bubble," a sheltered community which residents rarely ventured out of. Max (b. 1985, male, very externally-oriented) asserted that this insular mentality was shared amongst Chalmette residents, stating, "that um, mindset – like when you live in Chalmette, when you live in St. Bernard, how it's just like the whole world pretty much."[6] Others in the sample who had spent significant time outside of Chalmette – a marked behavior in St. Bernard Parish – discussed "bursting" that bubble by leaving Chalmette and having an epiphany about how sheltered their lives had been before. Roger (b. 1982, male, very externally oriented) reports that gaining this outsider perspective made him stand out from his Chalmette friends who lacked curiosity about the world outside their home parish, saying "once you get out of the, the bubble that is Chalmette life, and you get a taste of what the rest of the world is like, you want to embrace it, you know."[7]

As some explained to me, part of the reason many Chalmatians prefer to stay in their bubble is that Chalmette is socially ostracized elsewhere in Greater New Orleans:

> Sugar Magnolia (b. 1970, female, very externally-oriented): "My goal in high school was to move out of Chalmette. That was – it didn't matter what I was doing, I just didn't want to be in Chalmette. Because that was not cool. I was never going to live in Chalmette. Because there's just this stigma. You don't want that. You don't want to live in Chalmette."[8]

Notably, Sugar Magnolia is an individual who returned to Chalmette after the storm, despite her articulation of outsider judgments about Chalmette as stigmatized and uncool. That is, even with this awareness of negative associations, Chalmette retains value for its most loyal residents (and this loyalty in the face of stigmatization is often treated as a core feature of Chalmatian identity).

The negative and socially peripheralizing view of Chalmette can be seen in the circulation of visual memes characterizing Greater New Orleans. The town of Chalmette gets a particularly dismissive treatment from the judgmental maps meme, presented in Figure 4. Judgmental maps are a form of folk human geography, with individuals submitting to http://judgmentalmaps.com/ their

---

[5] Accompanying audio file Sound 4 is available at www.cambridge.org/EISO_Carmichael
[6] Accompanying audio file Sound 5 is available at www.cambridge.org/EISO_Carmichael
[7] Accompanying audio file Sound 6 is available at www.cambridge.org/EISO_Carmichael
[8] Accompanying audio file Sound 7 is available at www.cambridge.org/EISO_Carmichael

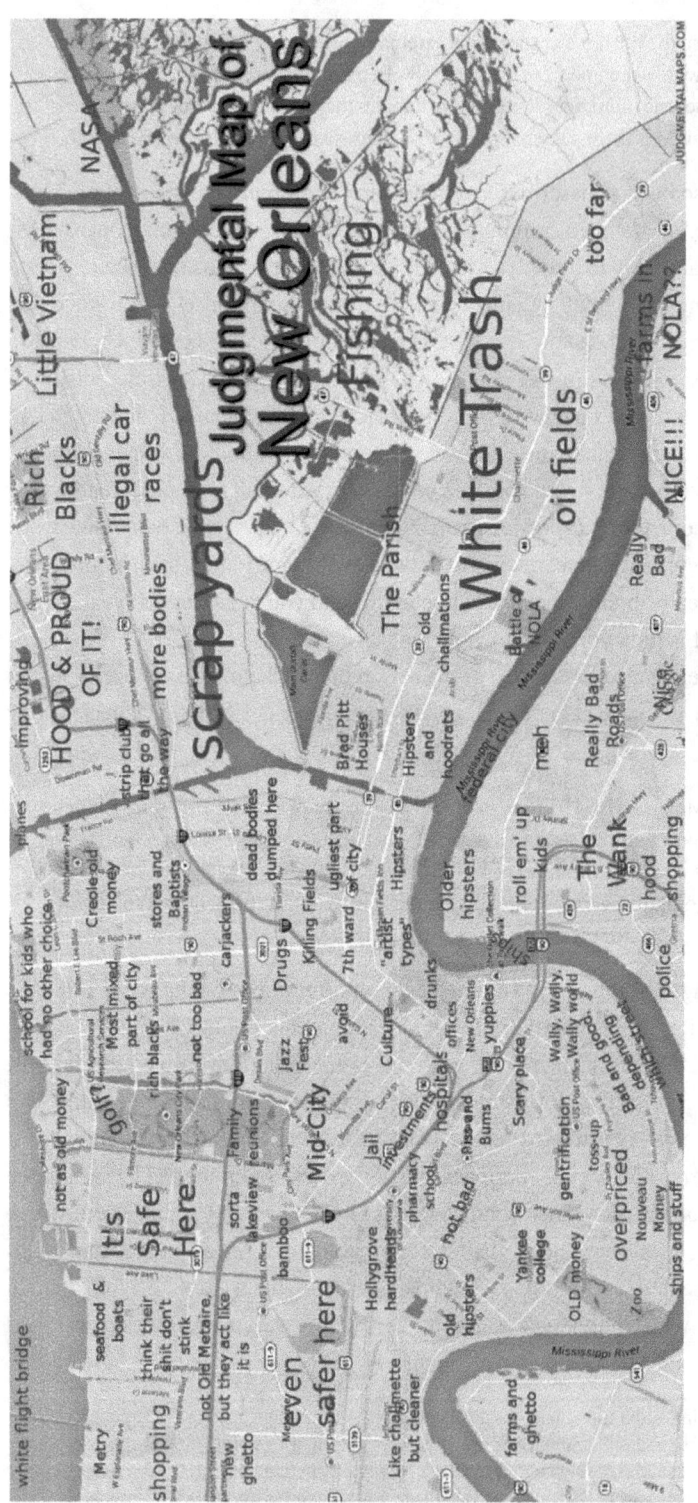

Figure 4 Judgmental map of New Orleans.

(**Source:** https://judgmentalmaps.com/post/98323841965/neworleans, last accessed August 4, 2023).

contemporary views of how space is divided within particular US cities (a selection of maps was published in 2016 by Trent Gillaspie in a book-length collection). While much of the commentary in these labels resembles simple snark about certain neighborhoods, one can also derive ideas about how different spaces and places are valued within a locale. For example, the label for Chalmette features the largest font label on this map, reading simply: "White Trash."

Though other suburban locations get multiple labels and descriptors, Chalmette is presented in an extremely simple, straightforward, and derisive way. It is almost as if Chalmette's reputation is so strong, that no more detail needs to be provided (or alternatively, that the map drawer has spent so little time in Chalmette that they do not have access to further details, negative or positive). Similarly, in perceptual dialectology map tasks completed documenting linguistic perceptions in Greater New Orleans, Chalmette is the most frequently marked locale, indicating equally strong (negative) stereotypes about language practices in the town (Dajko & Carmichael 2023), as well as ideologies about Chalmette's distinctness within the broader mental geography of the city. Continuing the theme of identifying Chalmette's undesirability and peripheral nature, Figure 5 presents a parody of Disney's *The Lion King* which circulated with various versions for different cities, often identifying dangerous or stigmatized neighborhoods. In this meme, Chalmette is described as outside the "kingdom" (presumably New Orleans proper in this case) and a "shadowy place" one "must never go" to.

Chalmatians are aware of these judgments, with Super (b. 1950, female, very Chalmette-oriented) stating, "you're always gonna have people that's gonna knock everything about the Parish down here."[9] JuAllison (b. 1979, female, very Chalmette-oriented) ties these judgments to the multivalent term 'Chalmatian,' which is sometimes used in a derisive way by outsiders, saying: "people do use it [the word Chalmatian] in a sense to be mean and ignorant and ugly. And it's the people who have never stepped a foot in Chalmette in their life!"[10] By stating that the people who use the label Chalmatian as an insult are also those without personal experience in Chalmette, she draws a line between those who have true ties to Chalmette as a place, and those who appeal to broader stereotypes; she thereby undermines the authority of these outsiders, noting that they do not have adequate experience to understand Chalmette as a place. Christian (b. 1963, male, somewhat externally-oriented) links the spatial and social peripheralization of Chalmette while describing a genre of Chalmatian jokes, "just like West Virginia is to Virginia, Mississippi is to Louisiana, Chalmette is to New Orleans metro, you know. So, you know,

---

[9] Accompanying audio file Sound 8 is available at www.cambridge.org/EISO_Carmichael
[10] Accompanying audio file Sound 9 is available at www.cambridge.org/EISO_Carmichael

Figure 5 Chalmette as shadowy place meme. (**Source**: http://www.quickmeme.com/meme/364b0v, last accessed September 25, 2020).

there was always kind of that stigma."[11] In this quote, we see certain locales centered (Virginia, Louisiana, and New Orleans metro), with peripheral locales (West Virginia, Mississippi, and Chalmette) existing only to be poked fun at.

In addition to spatial and social peripheralization, Chalmatians also experience linguistic marginalization. Indeed, parodies and memes centering on the Chalmette accent seem to nearly pathologize it. This can be seen, for example, in Figure 6 which features a photoshopped image circulating on social media, the cover of the language-learning computer program Rosetta Stone was doctored such that the language read: "Chalmation" [sic].

This meme *denaturalizes* (Bucholtz & Hall 2005) Chalmette residents' claims to local language by treating their linguistic practices as deviant – a foreign language, even. Similarly putting the accent's deviance in the spotlight has been the attention

---

[11] Accompanying audio file Sound 10 is available at www.cambridge.org/EISO_Carmichael

Figure 6 Chalmation [sic] Rosetta Stone.
(**Source**: https://www.pinterest.com/pin/429671620680112745/, last accessed October 5, 2023).

given to the playful 'Chalmette Hey Brah English-ish' add-on to the Waze driving app (MacCash 2023). By labeling this accent as 'English-ish,' it once again frames the accent as barely English. The add-on was indeed recorded by a Chalmette local, Shane Ansardi, who speaks with notable Yat linguistic features. In stark contrast to typically formal, standard-sounding GPS directions, the audio provides colorful commentary and nonstandard phrasing – for example, instead of saying 'turn left,' the voice says 'hook a leff,'[12] and if the driver does not follow instructions, requiring recalculation of the route, the voice says – with a notably r-less realization of 'Lord' and apical -ING: "oh lawd, reroutin', reroutin', here we go."[13] Both examples feature the inclusion of general nonstandard features not specific to Chalmette, like consonant cluster reduction and apical -ING, thereby emphasizing its general nonstandardness above and beyond traditional Yat features. The add-on has been celebrated across New Orleans as a playful joke that has spawned a number of social media posts, further reifying and othering Chalmatian ways of speaking, while granting authentic insider status to locals who 'get the joke.' Indeed, Fleurty Girl, one of the local Tee-shirt and souvenir shops that caters to

---

[12] Accompanying audio file Sound 11 is available at www.cambridge.org/EISO_Carmichael
[13] Accompanying audio file Sound 12 is available at www.cambridge.org/EISO_Carmichael

Figure 7 Fleurty Girl Instagram post with Shane Ansardi, the "Chalmette HeyBrah" voice on the Waze add-on.
(**Source**: www.fox8live.com/2023/08/06/chalmette-local-infuses-waze-navigation-with-homegrown-humor-charm/, last accessed October 6, 2023).

New Orleanians wishing to broadcast their insider knowledge via their shirt, mug, tea towel, or coasters posted a photo to Instagram of the owner alongside add-on creator Ansardi. Figure 7 presents a screen capture of the post, shared in one of the numerous articles lauding the add-on.

The article goes on to state that the add-on "gives a new spin to the typical navigation experience, making each drive feel closer to home, regardless of where you might be headed" (FOX8 Staff 2023). This drives the point home (pun intended) that this accent – especially in disembodied form – is locally viewed as 'belonging to' New Orleanians (as part of the soundscape that defines their home), and appreciated in specifically performative environments (especially when the voice can be turned off at the touch of a button).

Language and Place 51

5.5 Authenticity, Performance, and Peripheralization in Post-Katrina New Orleans

5.5.1 Place and Placelessness in Greater New Orleans

New Orleans has always been "a city not only which visitors find 'unique' but a city whose residents have a strongly developed sense of themselves, a mindset which stems in part from an awareness of participating in a distinctive urban folk culture" (de Caro 1992: 71–72). This can be seen, in part, in the marketing of New Orleans, which centers on selling the distinctive food, music, and traditions of the city as a part of the massive tourism industry. However, not all of the commodification is outward-facing – in particular, since Hurricane Katrina in 2005, the city has seen a flurry of shops opening that sell Tee-shirts and other home goods which represent local sayings and other markers of insider knowledge (Schoux Casey 2013; Carmichael & Dajko 2016). These items are one way of performing this locally authentic, insider persona, and also of demonstrating one's self-awareness of the city's unique qualities. For example, in Figure 8 we see that the French Quarter store Forever New Orleans, which opened in 2007, sells kitchen towels, signs, and Tee-shirts with the Tennessee Williams quote, "America has only three cities: New York, San Francisco, and New Orleans. Everywhere else is Cleveland."

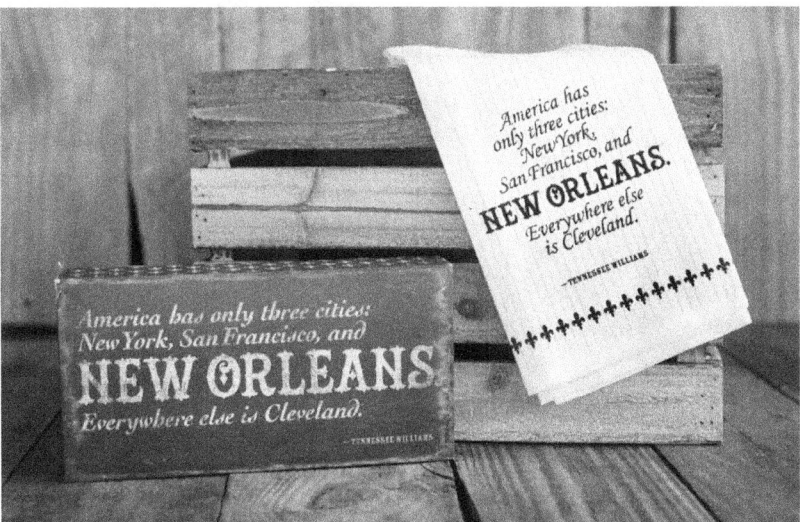

Figure 8 Tennessee Williams sign and tea towel from Forever New Orleans. (**Source**: https://shopforeverneworleans.com/product/tennessee-williams-quote-kitchen-towel/, last accessed June 22, 2021).

Thus we see New Orleans' "place-iness" on display, and everywhere else pointed to as placeless; soulless; cultureless; bland – Cleveland. Some of this performance comes through the display of Tee-shirts and other merchandise that commodifies the Yat accent and distinctive local phrases, as has happened in locales (Heller 2003; Johnstone 2009, 2010b). Of these goods, Schoux Casey (2013: 142) writes, "New Orleans language-decorated merchandise functions as both a symbol of local pride and insider knowledge, and as a nostalgic emblem of localness." Some examples of this come from the frequently commodified local phrase "making groceries" (to go grocery shopping) seen in Figure 9.

Awareness and performance of local linguistic features became a marker, post-Katrina, of the New Orleanians "born and raised" in the area, in contrast with newcomers. Following the storm, a significant portion of the pre-Katrina population was permanently displaced, however, a secondary form of displacement came in the form of gentrification – a problem not specific to New Orleans, but which has occurred with an extreme and visible rapidity in the city following the storm. These 'gentrifying' transplants are perceived as mostly white, mostly wealthy, and drawn to the unique culture of the city – and indeed, since there is so much performativity to being New Orleanian, there are many linguistic and cultural traditions for an outsider to acquire. However, there has

Figure 9 Making groceries bag, shirt, and notepad.
(**Source**: bag, Fleurty Girl www.fleurtygirl.net/bag-makin-groceries-tote.html, last accessed June 22, 2021). (**Source**: shirt, Home Malone https://homemalonenola.com/products/makingroceriestee, last accessed June 22, 2021). (**Source**: notepad, Dirty Coast https://dirtycoast.com/products/makin-groceries-notepad, last accessed June 22, 2021).

been significant pushback from longstanding locals against 'fake' New Orleanians, these recent post-Katrina transplants seeking to participate in, and appropriate, local traditions, who are thus sometimes contemptuously referred to as 'culture vultures.' In particular, the idea of the white transplant 'hipster' living in the newly gentrified French-Quarter-adjacent Marigny and Bywater neighborhoods has become a common trope representative of a particular kind of appropriative identity in the city (Dajko & Carmichael 2023). Cultural gentrification has accompanied the literal gentrification happening in post-Katrina New Orleans, which has been studied with respect to secondline parades, a cultural tradition of Black New Orleans which have been infiltrated and appropriated by white transplants and tourists (Schoux Casey 2020). As these unique-to-New-Orleans traditions have become commodified, they have also become more accessible to outsiders, who are framed by locals as culture-less and placeless. In Bucholtz and Hall's (2005) terms, these outsiders are all *adequated* into a single "from elsewhere" category, or as one perceptual dialectology map-drawer from Dajko & Carmichael (2023) asked to circle where areas of the city had changed linguistically post-Katrina put it: "I'm from anywhere" hipsters (Figure 10).

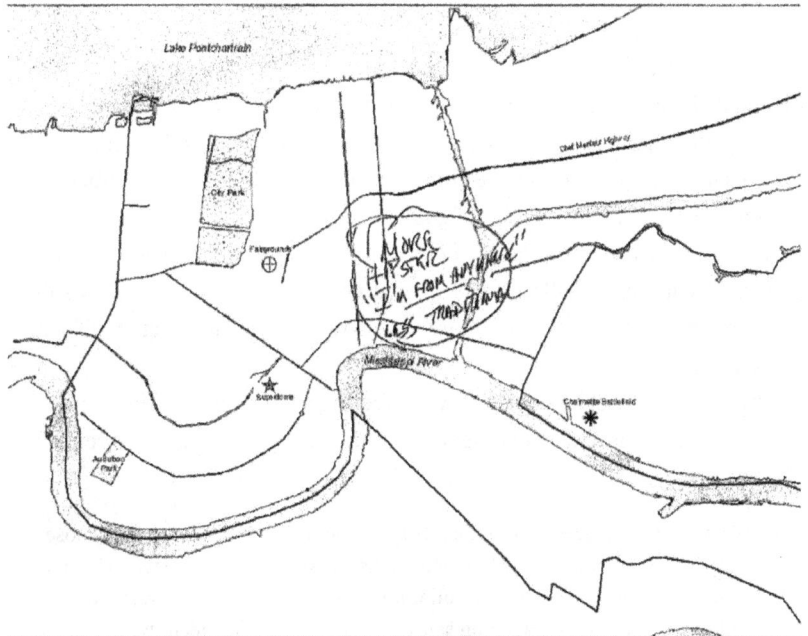

Figure 10 Perceptual dialectology map – post-Katrina changes highlighting "I'm from anywhere" hipsters.

In the words of Tennessee Williams, these newcomer hipsters are "from Cleveland," which is equivalent to being from nowhere, insofar as cultural and linguistic cachet goes. In many ways, Hurricane Katrina has initiated a process of revaluing of the local, in New Orleans, as the residents who returned post-Katrina grieve a version of the city from before the storm (Carmichael & Dajko 2016) – but even more than that, they cling to the belief that remembering these linguistic markers of a lost city can help them retain what is unique and authentic about New Orleans in the face of the placeless newcomers who are replacing large swaths of the city's population. Put in terms of Bucholtz & Hall's (2005) sociocultural framework: lifelong residents of the city *distinguish* themselves from these transplants, and *authenticate* themselves as longstanding New Orleanians, by displaying their insider knowledge of traditional practices – including language use.

But longstanding residents of Greater New Orleans are also subject to these same processes. 'Authentic' New Orleans is defined based in large part on a "Disneyfied" version of the city since "as New Orleanians embraced tourism, they reinforced, as the city's focal point, the *Vieux Carré*" or French Quarter (Souther 2007: 805). Part of this place-making is visual – architectural. In Figure 11, we see the prototypical Disneyfied French Quarter, with its wrought iron lace balconies and bright Caribbean paint colors.

Most of the city, of course, does not resemble the historic French Quarter, though it is true that throughout New Orleans neighborhoods there are many distinctively local architectural components, such as large front porches and bright paint colors, shotgun-style homes and Creole cottages. In contrast, in the suburbs many of the homes were built as post-war brick bungalows, practical and cheaply made, without historic significance nor architectural distinction. The roads are wide and multi-laned, betraying their post-automobile construction, and lined with strip malls instead of live oaks. Indeed, New Orleans suburbs are "anywhere" suburbs, as Figure 12 shows a typical street in Chalmette demonstrates.

This idea of placelessness deriving feelings of angst – or, in contrast, no feelings at all – is well documented within human geography. Arefi (2013: 296) writes:

> We remember places that invoke different emotions in us better than those that look the same (i.e., shopping malls or strip developments). Certain landscapes tend to be more meaningful to us than others; we prefer to live and work in areas with a strong sense of place and unique identity.

Of course, this does not mean that Chalmette's landscape is not meaningful to its residents (in fact I would argue the contrary), but more so that it is easily framed

Language and Place 55

Figure 11 Disneyfied NOLA (photo by Katie Carmichael).

as such by outsiders; as Rapoport (1977: 215) aptly puts it: "what is dull to an outsider may be rich to the native." Thus, as Chalmatians fit into the suburb-as-nowhere paradigm, their status as authentic New Orleanians could never be ratified, no matter how many generations back they go, or how many traditional local linguistic features they use.

5.5.2 A Place in Time: Nostalgia Culture and the Power of the Past

Nostalgia for a place-linked way of speaking is not specific to New Orleans, rather it is a broader trend across the United States as patterns of homogenization and standardization are seen as threatening the sense of place for urban and rural locales alike (Relph 1976; Arefi 1999, 2013). Silverstein (2014) writes of this ache for regional linguistic peculiarities, comparing local accents to *terroir* in wine culture, writing that "like '*appellation d'origine contrôlée*' of one's wine, identifiable geographically connected accent, too, has become a positive

Figure 12 Typical Chalmette street.
(**Source**: Google Street view: www.google.com/maps/@29.9338766,-89.9535104,
3a,75y,208.9h,97.59t/data=!3m7!1e1!3m5!1sxwkZ2rGvcY3Cg4Xplbd4VA!
2e0!6shttps:%2F%2Fstreetviewpixels-pa.googleapis.com%2Fv1%2
Fthumbnail%3Fpanoid%3DxwkZ2rGvcY3Cg4Xplbd4VA%26cb_client%3
Dsearch.revgeo_and_fetch.gps%26w%3D96%26h%3D64%26yaw%3D287
.41116%26pitch%3D0%26thumbfov%3D100!7i16384!8i8192?entry=ttu, last
accessed May 30, 2023).

emblem of a sense of placèdness" (Silverstein 2014: 183). Silverstein focuses on the New York City accent, acknowledging (as a native Brooklynite himself) that the deictic center of the accent for speakers has expanded outward to the boroughs, as the island of Manhattan itself has priced out many of the working class speakers who speak this way. Becker & Newlin-Lukowicz (2018) demonstrate via a perception task that New Yorkers themselves are aware of this connection between the outer boroughs and increased accentedness, and yet ideologically, the accent remains tied to the city-center of Manhattan. That is, as in New Orleans, as gentrification has claimed the urban core for the monied elite, the working class individuals who use local linguistic features in a genuine, non-performative manner are pushed farther to the (physical) periphery, and then lamented in the abstract form – when they are no longer present to provide the grounding in place. Providing an apt metaphor for this depersonalization of language from speakers, Silverstein (2014: 179) writes:

> [People] seem to think of this disappearance [of regional dialects] as like the decline of endangered species in the natural landscape. Hence, one has to travel to the outer urban reaches still to find it, where somehow its habitat has not been destroyed, a kind of temporality-laden ethno-theory of relic areas not yet penetrated by modernity's standardization, perhaps.

Notably, in this analysis, Silverstein nods to the time dimension as well as the physical, geographic peripheralization of these speakers; not only are they spatially peripheralized in present day, but they are erased entirely from the picture as they are treated as relics of a past version of the city – as Carmichael & Dajko (2016) have argued, a chronotopic sense of New Orleans as a place. That is, authenticity is tied to both a place *and* a time. In that way, the only way to successfully achieve ratified linguistic authenticity is to do so performatively. In their current status as existing within the present, and in the geographic periphery to New Orleans, Chalmatians have claim to neither the correct place nor time. As a result, despite their use of the very linguistic features being commodified and celebrated in post-Katrina New Orleans, they are denied the role of "authentic New Orleanian."

The linkage between the Yat accent and New Orleans as a place has only intensified following Hurricane Katrina and the physical upheaval that the storm caused (Mucciaccio 2009; Carmichael 2017). Linguistic commodification and nostalgia culture after the storm has resulted in some detachment of the features from the actual speakers of Yat themselves, as Schoux Casey (2016: 149) describes:

> Language and other cultural objects that are fading away, or have disappeared, are in an ideal state to be recontextualized as appropriate objects of nostalgia and commodification. This is because they are freed from their former attachments to living, specific and complex groups of people, whose authority as speakers might challenge the new, often simplistic social meanings being attached to particular features.

Schoux Casey notes that the reification of Yat ways of speaking allows for its commodification as a part of nostalgia culture in the city; that is, the enregisterment of this dialect as a "thing" – and a specifically place-linked thing – is an essential first step to its employment as a tool for expressing authenticity, rootedness, and ties to a past version of the city. Since Hurricane Katrina, increased mobility into and out of New Orleans has magnified the distinction between locals and non-locals. Longstanding locals authenticate themselves via the employment of these enregistered linguistic features. However, the linguistic features pointed to as signs of authentic localness tend to be those that have risen to the level of stereotype – the very features that locals have shifted away from in everyday use due to stigma. Their employment of older linguistic features indexes the feeling of nostalgia for a New Orleans where Hurricane Katrina had not yet occurred, and when Yat features were heard in the city center – but it also erases remaining everyday users of Yat features who now live on the periphery of the city itself.

Thus, just as the spatial deictic center of Yat is in New Orleans proper, not in Chalmette, the temporal referent for Yat is in the past, not in the present. This particular triangulation of space-time purposely excludes any new arrivals to the city, identifying them as inauthentic poseurs, but it also renders contemporary users of Yat linguistic features – Chalmatians – invisible and illegible within this frame (Carmichael & Dajko 2016). Modan (2007: 148) similarly noted that in the neighborhood of Mt. Pleasant in Washington, D.C., certain individuals were identified as "out of place" and denied legitimate claims to the neighborhood, as residents staked a claim to Mt. Pleasant by defining its identity as a place (and thereby staking their authority as an individual who could identify what 'type' of person belongs, and who does not).

5.5.3 Fractal Recursivity and the Cline of Authenticity in Greater New Orleans

Given the local revaluing of traditional New Orleans linguistic features described above, it seems only logical that the pinnacle of authentic New Orleans identity would be the 'modern-day Yats' found in Chalmette. Yet, as we have seen, these individuals remain socially, geographically, and linguistically peripheralized. The resulting scenario resembles that which Leeman & Modan (2010) found in their examination of commodified DC Chinatown, in which visual imagery was appropriated from the past, ultimately erasing the current Chinese Americans the occupied that space, whose authenticity was challenged by the corporatized visual representations of Chinese-ness. Likewise, Chalmatians, in contrast with their valorized language use in commodified forms, continue to be marginalized by the very New Orleanians who perform these features in a show of localness to distinguish themselves as having a stronger claim to the city of New Orleans.

Irvine & Gal (2000: 38) introduce the concept of 'fractal recursivity,' writing that "fractal recursivity involves the projection of an opposition on some level of relationship, onto some other level […] the myriad oppositions that create identity may be reproduced repeatedly, either within each side of a dichotomy or outside it." Borrowing from this concept, Dajko & Carmichael (2023) describe how within Greater New Orleans, contrasts are drawn between suburban Yats (including Chalmatians) and residents of New Orleans proper, in terms of who gets to claim authentic ties to the city; then this contrast repeats on a smaller scale within New Orleans itself, in the battle between longstanding New Orleanians and transplants. In both cases, language features prominently in the struggle for recognition as A True New Orleanian. In Figure 13, I conceptualize this in terms of what I call the Cline of Local Authenticity, which accounts for factors of place, time, language practices, and performativity, capturing the reasons that newcomer transplants *and* Chalmatians will always retain marginal claims to an authentically New Orleanian identity.

Language and Place

While both Chalmatians and lifelong New Orleanians feature a time-depth in the region that exceeds that of the transplant, lifelong New Orleanians additionally feature geographic ties to the city proper, rather than peripheral areas. When speaking standardly, these lifelong New Orleanians have superiority to the linguistically deviant Chalmatians, and when performatively using Yat features, they have superiority to the "from anywhere" transplants who do not have adequate awareness of these features to perform them appropriately. Thus, regardless of the 'linguistic match-up,' lifelong New Orleanians who can perform Yat features at will – and also erase them from their speech when it suits them – claim linguistic superiority to those around them. This can't-win situation for Chalmatians denies them any possibility of claiming an authentic New Orleanian identity. This is the joke central to the meme presented in Figure 14 which points out that while Chalmatians will always claim New Orleans, New Orleanians will never claim Chalmette.

With this meme we see the uneven power relationship between New Orleans and Chalmette, and the supposed superior desirability of New Orleans over Chalmette. But we also see that, from the perspective of Chalmatians, their linguistic features can index both a Chalmette- and a New Orleans-linked identity – both are equally valid and relevant. But for New-Orleans-Centered residents, only Yat features used performatively by those spatially tied to the city center are considered authentically New Orleanian.

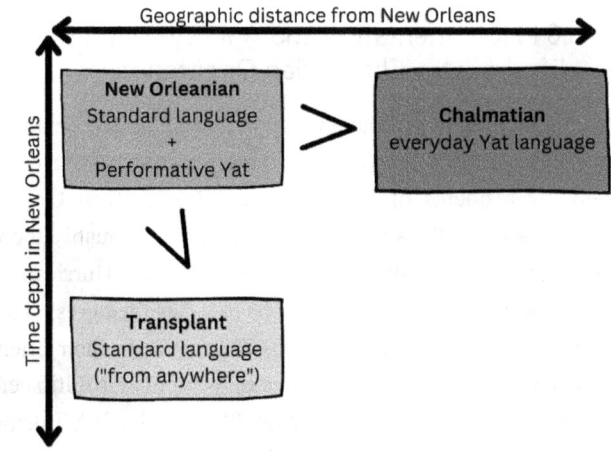

Figure 13 The Cline of Local Authenticity in post-Katrina New Orleans.

Figure 14 Chalmette and New Orleans meme.
(**Source**: https://www.reddit.com/r/NewOrleans/comments/mzfn8a/_/, last accessed October 2, 2023).

5.6 Place Orientation and Agency: The Case of Extra-Chalmatian Orientation

Above, I have argued that Chalmatian ways of speaking are denigrated when used in everyday speech by residents of Chalmette, but valorized when used performatively by residents of other parts of Greater New Orleans. Since Chalmatians are aware of the stigma of their accents – arguably more so than ever, given their increased exposure to outsiders following Hurricane Katrina – the question arises: why do they continue to use these features? The answer, I have argued (cf. Carmichael 2017, 2020, 2023), lies in their orientation to a Chalmette-centric identity. Via the development of a Multifaceted Place Orientation Metric (MPOM; see Carmichael 2023 for details), I demonstrated that for traditional Yat features like nonrhoticity and split short-a systems, participants with the highest extra-Chalmatian orientation score – those most oriented toward places *outside of* Chalmette – are those *least* likely to use the locally marked features. That is, Chalmatians who continue to use these stigmatized features are actively orienting toward an Insider lens of these features, and indeed of Chalmatian identity on the whole.

In her work on gentrifying Anacostia in Washington, DC, Grieser (2022) outlines Insider Discourses and Outsider Discourses about gentrification, and the ways these discourses came into direct conflict in the neighborhood as locals mobilized both in their construction of Anacostia as a place. I argue that, similarly, in Chalmette residents demonstrate keen awareness of Insider versus Outsider Discourses about Chalmatian identity and their claims to New Orleans as a city. In use of marked, Yatty features like nonrhoticity and split short-a systems, Chalmatian English speakers are orienting toward Insider norms and rejecting the Outsider definitions of Chalmatian identity – as trashy, unworldly, and ignorant. The question then arises – what is the insider view of Chalmette?

Chalmatians interviewed for this study described Chalmette as neighborly, laidback, tight-knit, and friendly. One frequently repeated genre of story I heard repeatedly is what I call the Grocery Store Story. In this narrative mode, participants described grocery store visits as a long affair in which you ran into all your neighbors and cousins and friends and had to check in about "your momma and 'em" (an iconically Yat phrase in the city which has also been commodified). Crucially, this story genre was also used to mark places outside of Chalmette as *different* from other locales that Chalmatians experienced after Katrina, either as temporary evacuees (Molly) or permanently relocated residents (Chocolate):

> Molly (b. 1989, female, very Chalmette-oriented): "Down here [in Chalmette] you can walk into the grocery store and know like ten people, and everybody's gonna talk and ask you how your day was, what's going on, how's everybody. When you, like, when we were in Baton Rouge [after evacuating], they just – it's a different breed, I don't know. They just don't, they don't care what you're doing, they don't care about your life. Down here, everybody cares."[14]

> Chocolate (b. 1959, female, very Chalmette-oriented): "It was different up here [in the Northshore suburbs], it was, you know, starting over and, and going to the grocery store and not seeing people that you ... recognized – I'm sorry, I'm getting a little emotional here. Um, that was kind of tough, it was weird, you know."[15]

In these examples, both Baton Rouge and the Northshore of Lake Pontchartrain are marked as different from Chalmette – less caring, less tight-knit. Notably, these

---

[14] Accompanying audio file Sound 13 is available at www.cambridge.org/EISO_Carmichael
[15] Accompanying audio file Sound 14 is available at www.cambridge.org/EISO_Carmichael

speakers attribute these qualities to the place itself, not to their own newcomer/ outsider status during the time spent in these areas. Many participants – returners and relocators alike – also indicated experiencing stigmatization for their Chalmatian accent and identity following the storm, with outsiders linking Chalmatian identity to stereotypes about being lower class, trashy, and uneducated:

> Sugar Magnolia (b. 1970, female, very externally-oriented): "The stigma of being from St. Bernard Parish when I was young was always, um ... people in St. Bernard Parish are less educated. They're those uh, blue collar worker people."[16]
>
> Christian (b. 1963, male, somewhat externally-oriented): "[Outsider judgments of Chalmette were that] this was always more trailer park-y and, you know, a little more lower class type of people."[17]

Notably, the positive (insider) and negative (outsider) associations with Chalmatian identity – and thus Chalmatian ways of speaking – circulate together, forming an indexical field (Eckert 2008) with low status, high solidarity values, common for vernacular speech varieties (Luhman 1990). Figure 15 presents some of these aspects of the indexical field, noting the 'insider' versus 'outsider' interpretations of these features.

Chalmatians, in their construction of place identity, embrace the components of the Chalmatian English indexical field that fit their worldview, and acknowledge but reject the outsiders' judgments. Outsiders, in turn, do not validate the claim of Chalmatian English speakers to these positive aspects of the indexical field – though they validate these same associations when the dialect is used performatively by those with New-Orleans-center claims. Thus by using

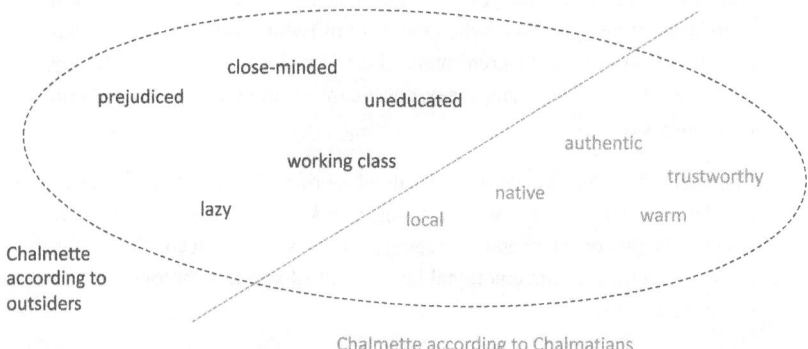

Figure 15 Chalmatian English indexical field.

---

[16] Accompanying audio file Sound 15 is available at www.cambridge.org/EISO_Carmichael
[17] Accompanying audio file Sound 16 is available at www.cambridge.org/EISO_Carmichael

Chalmatian English features in the face of external judgment, Chalmatians indirectly index their orientation toward an insider worldview, and their rejection of external viewpoints (Carmichael 2023). Without place theory, we might be able to draw conclusions about social class or covert prestige, but we would be missing the broader significance of place-based identity in Greater New Orleans, especially as Hurricane Katrina has highlighted the importance of place in this post-disaster landscape.

5.7 Conclusions

As Eble (2006: 46) writes, "Local identity is a performance art in New Orleans." This performativity is reinforced by ideologies about who, within this space, has a right to such identities, and how spatial and geographic peripheralization contributes to such beliefs. The traditional New Orleans accent is intrinsically linked to local imaginings of pre-Katrina New Orleans, and indexes long-term ties to the city. Through the performance of the local dialect, lifelong residents are able to assert their authentic claims to New Orleans, in contrast with newcomer populations arriving from out of state. Intriguingly, however, the very individuals in the city – Chalmatians – who continue to use local linguistic features in a non-performative way remain peripheralized.

In this analysis, I have demonstrated the ways that Chalmette is framed as a peripheral place within Greater New Orleans, via examples of its geographic, social, and linguistic peripheralization. Outside of Chalmette, Chalmatians are consistently denied their claims to being authentic ratified New Orleanians, even as their speech patterns reflect the traditional linguistic features that have been commodified more broadly as THE expression of locality and pre-Katrina rootedness. The patterns of marginalization and othering seen in memes about Chalmette and Chalmatian ways of speaking demonstrate how the peripherality of certain groups can undermine their claims even to their own language practices. Yet, as Chalmatians persist in using their locally marked ways of speaking, they agentively reject this indexical interpretation of their speech, opting instead to identify with their self-defined version of place identity despite awareness of external framings of their home.

6 The Evocation of a Stigmatized Place: Hollering the Holler

6.1 Introduction

As the previous sections have outlined – *place* and how speakers feel about place matters. The present analysis aims to show how *place* is crucial to understanding how speakers both recognize and use linguistic forms, some stereotyped and caricatured, in the face of marginalization from both outsiders and insiders and maintain some aspects of varieties (or potentially change) (cf. Ryan 1979). Via qualitative analysis, this section identifies themes in the ways East Tennessee Appalachian English (AE) speakers describe their linguistic ideologies and tie them to their homeplace. In the process, one can see that a speaker's relationship to place can override any circulating negative stereotype and encourage the use of linguistic features specifically tied to place.

Appalachia is the mountainous region in the Eastern and Southeastern United States that stretches from northern Georgia to Pennsylvania (ARC 2015). It is distinctive from other parts of the American South culturally and linguistically, with local speech varieties, broadly referred to as 'Appalachian Englishes' (Hazen 2020), that diverge from Mainstream American English and other Southern American English varieties (Pederson, McDaniel, & Adams 1986–93; Carver 1987; Labov, Ash, & Boberg 2006, among others), and crucially, are not internally monolithic. In fact, akin to all regions and language varieties, there is much internal variation in both culture and speech. Across the region, a strong sense of regional identity exists (Jones 1994; Reed 2018a; inter alia) that is reflected in the linguistic practices of speakers from the region. Yet there is scant scholarly work on the ideologies underlying evaluations of these varieties by native AE speakers. Cramer (2018) compares and contrasts the perceptual dialectology maps of college students in Kentucky, showing how both natives and non-natives hold notions, both positive and negative, about the region. This perceptual dialectological work echoes findings from more earlier matched guise perceptual work (Luhman 1990). Here, he finds circulating stereotypes about speakers from Eastern Kentucky, which natives to the region understand and sometimes reflect with respect to prestige and status, but, crucially, often reject with respect to the social and solidarity components of perception. The present work focuses on a small rural community in northeast Tennessee and illuminates how speakers convey and respond to a local place-based identity. Furthermore, we see how speakers from Appalachia discursively position themselves with respect to circulating tropes and stigmas.

Prior work focused on this area (Reed 2016, 2018a, 2018b, 2020a, 2020b) argues that speakers in the region construct this locally and regionally place-based identity (or identities) through their speech, demonstrating crucially that speakers in this community have differing levels of place-attachment, that is, *rootedness*, and these differing levels of rootedness are predictive for certain linguistic practices (see description of quantifications of place above in Section 3.6). Some speakers are highly attached to place, and thus are strongly rooted. Other speakers are less strongly attached to place and are less rooted. These rootedness differences surface in linguistic production (see Section 6.4 for elaboration). The question remains, however, what role these factors play in linguistic perception. The present section shows how speakers who are more or less rooted discuss their region and language, demonstrating that an attachment to place matters.

6.2 Place in the History of Tennessee

Any discussion of *place* in Tennessee necessitates some background of the state itself, as *place* and geography features prominently in state history, particularly for East Tennessee which is the focus of this study. The following sections outline the Grand Divisions of the state, explain why the Divisions arose, and then focus on East Tennessee and, in particular, Upper East Tennessee, and explore why *place* and its perception are so meaningful in this subregion.

Tennessee is somewhat unusual among states in the United States in that it has officially recognized and sanctioned Grand Divisions: East, Middle, and West Tennessee (see Figures 16–18).

Each division contains roughly one-third of the state's land area. The counties that comprise each Division are specified by state law (State of Tennessee 2015). The Grand Divisions are reflected in the state flag, where the three central stars represent the Grand Divisions (see Figure 19).

The Grand Divisions roughly equate to differences in geography, rugosity, and elevation, and some geographical features have been declared borders.[18] East Tennessee is mountainous. Fertile valleys and lightly rolling landscapes characterize most of Middle Tennessee. The westernmost Grand Division is flatter and lower-lying and part of the expansive Gulf Coastal Plain region. Its character is level, fertile ground, quite suitable for large-scale agriculture.

The sectionalism of Tennessee and formally recognized Grand Divisions have implications in state governance. For example, on the Tennessee Supreme Court, there can be no more than two justices of the five members of the Court from any single Grand Division and the court must hold a session in each Division during each session term. (State of Tennessee 2015). Thus, *place* has an impact even on state administration.

The differences between the Grand Divisions go deeper than even geography and governance. A perceived cultural difference also exists. Within the past thirty years, signs on interstates welcomed visitors to the 'Three States of Tennessee.' While gone now, such a motto reveals that the residents of the three Grand Divisions see themselves as not necessarily being unified. Crawford (1986: 63) notes, "the residents of these Grand Divisions have

---

[18] A 'clear' border between East and Middle Tennessee remains elusive. Further, some counties have passed from one division to the other. Most recently, Perry County has moved from West to Middle in 1991 (State of Tennessee 2015).

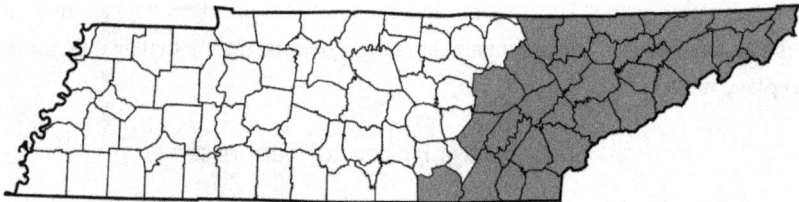

Figure 16 The counties of East Tennessee.

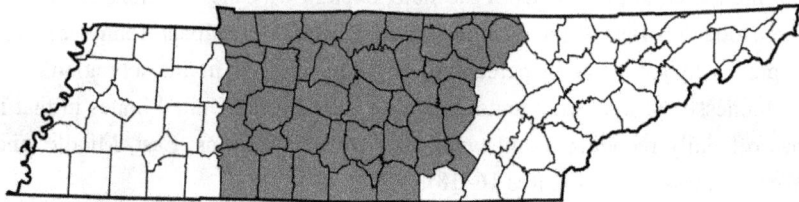

Figure 17 The counties of Middle Tennessee.

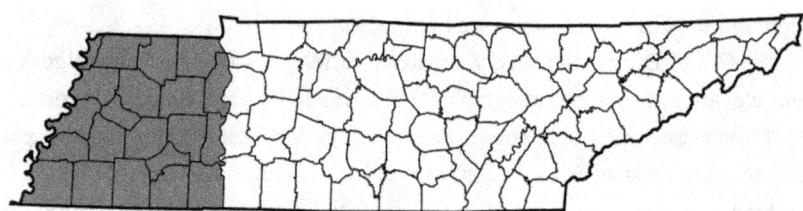

Figure 18 The counties of West Tennessee.

Figure 19 The flag of the state of Tennessee.

generally been, at a basic level, competitors when not enemies of one another. They are divided by a social and economic background of a different nature – more than by miles, even though the difference is great." This sectionalism has roots in the state's history.

Settlers first crossed the mountains from North Carolina and began to settle in the valleys of East Tennessee. As the population grew and treaties were signed with Native American nations, settlers continued to move west, where the land was flatter and richer. This more fertile land in the western portions of Tennessee facilitated larger-scale agriculture. As a result, plantation culture and a type of white Southern aristocracy took hold in what is now West Tennessee. Here, the climate and land were suited to growing cotton on large plantations with the labor of enslaved Africans. West Tennessee's economy grew to depend on cotton and this labor. In Middle Tennessee, there were fewer plantations, although there was still a burgeoning plantation culture based on tobacco, another labor-intensive crop requiring involuntary slave labor, and other large-scale agricultural practices, such as hog farming. However, in the East, the land was ill-suited for large-scale plantation work and most agriculture occurred on smaller plots of land; thus, plantation culture did not develop in this area (Bergeron, Ash, & Keith 1999; Tennessee Blue Book 2013). These booming slave-based economies shifted power and influence westward in the state. Naturally, the more populous East resented this, and called for splitting the state. To maintain a sense of cohesion and to attempt to avoid sectional crises, the 1834 State Constitution formally recognized the three grand divisions. Yet, critical differences remained, and were exacerbated by the Civil War, which saw the East remain allied with the Union, whereas Middle and West Tennessee were aligned with the Confederacy.

The shift of political and economic power, combined with differing views toward slavery and secession, consolidated the sectionalism feelings in Tennessee. This historical background provides context for why *place* features prominently for many people – mountain versus delta, wealthy and impoverished, secessionist and union. Where one lived mattered and shaped views toward one's fellow Tennesseans, and there were rather clear divisions between people based on *place*. This history began to imbue particular places with meaning, such as East Tennessee being different and separate. Thus, *place* was linked with identity, as different geographical areas (East TN vs Middle/West TN) were strongly linked with different perspectives.

6.3 Place in East Tennessee

The sense of separateness, and perhaps even uniqueness, embedded in the fabric of East Tennessee inspired many attempts to be recognized as independent and formally distinct. In fact, some say that place-identity features more prominently in East Tennessee than anywhere else in the state. As observed by Crawford (1986: 68), "it has been traditional in the mountain counties to view those of different experience and culture as real or potential enemies. And the local residents [of East

Tennessee] make little distinction between Middle and West Tennessee. All are outsiders ... " (see also Montgomery 1995). Such sentiments derive in part from historical realities and their interpretation. Tom Lee writes "political and economic disputes with the other sections of Tennessee produced among East Tennesseans a distinctive sectional identity built around a mythologized historical narrative of heroism and victimization that East Tennesseans themselves fostered and that persisted through the Civil War and into the twentieth century" (Lee 2010: 294). In fact, historian John Inscoe argues that the stronger regional identity in East Tennessee is what allowed for the stronger pro-Union sentiment in East Tennessee, in contrast to other mountain areas such as western North Carolina (Inscoe 2008: 103–123). The community perspective, memory, and identity in East Tennessee have been impacted by a somewhat unique history, and that community memory helps to mark *place* as something very important to East Tennesseans, and in particular, Upper East Tennesseans.

The roots of the belief that East Tennessee is different begin with the Battle of Kings Mountain in 1780 during the American Revolution, where a large group of East Tennessee militia, later known as the Overmountain Men, helped turn the tide by defeating the British near King's Mountain, NC. The regionality was a cause célèbre. Related, the regional identity played a key role in the short-lived State of Franklin, which seceded from North Carolina in 1784. North Carolina voted in 1784 to cede the land from the mountains to the Mississippi river to Congress to help offset war debts. Naturally, the settlers living in this region were not terribly pleased with this proposal. Some of the inhabitants of what is now East Tennessee formed their own state in 1784. The newly formed state petitioned the U.S. Congress for statehood, and was denied. Thus, the State of Franklin declared itself independent, and functioned as a separate entity until its dissolution and re-entry as a part of North Carolina in 1789 (Tennessee Blue Book 2013: 495). This separatist sentiment never fully left East Tennessee and bubbled to the surface many times in the decades following statehood in 1796. There were several proposals in the antebellum period for East Tennessee independence, stemming from the political power shifting to Middle and West Tennessee with the rise of the plantation aristocracy. These proposals were typically stalled, but the sectionalist differences continued. For example, a majority of the Tennessee citizenry voted to secede from the Union, but over 69 percent of the voters in East Tennessee opposed secession.[19] As a reaction against pro-secession forces from Middle and West Tennessee (and some counties in East Tennessee), the pro-Unionist East Tennessee Convention

---

[19] This total was actually down from the initial vote of 81 percent opposed to secession in the first statewide convention to consider leaving the Union. There were two conventions in 1861, one in February and the decisive one in June. The latter decision caused Tennessee to become the eleventh and final state to join the Confederacy.

convened in 1861 to petition the Tennessee state government and the federal government to allow East Tennessee to form a separate state, a 'mountain republic' (akin to the successful separatist movement in Virginia that led to the formation of West Virginia) (Kelley 2012). The state government denied this petition, and anti-East Tennessee sentiment (which was in reality anti-Unionist) ran high. As a result of this petition, East Tennessee was occupied by Confederate forces, and was not 'freed' until late 1863 (Lee 2010: 303–304).

The harsh response to the separatist movement has lived on in the memory of many and affected the perception of East Tennessee as well. From the sectional differences and the violent reaction, "antebellum perceptions of East Tennessee as a distinctive section within Tennessee evolved into a perception of East Tennessee as a distinctive region within the South" (Lee 2010: 294). For decades after the Civil War, its aftermath, and Reconstruction, East Tennessee viewed the rest of the state suspiciously and vice versa and was politically distinct (although this political distinction is now largely gone). The political contrast was known as 'Mountain Republicanism,'[20] in contrast to the 'Solid South,' which was almost uniformly Democrat. For example, a state guidebook on Tennessee produced by the Work Projects Administration in 1939 declared "To the East Tennessean, West Tennessee is almost as far away and unknown as Missouri. He looks upon the western section as a swamp and resents the weight of the powerful Shelby County political machine in state-wide elections. What West Tennessee is for, he is 'agin'" (WPA 1939: 4, as quoted in Montgomery 1995: 72). In 1959 and again in 1961, future U.S. Congressman James H. Quillen, while serving as a state legislator, proposed to the state legislature to resurrect the State of Franklin. One of his first acts as U.S. Congressman in 1963 was to propose that East Tennessee become the 51st state. Naturally, this was rejected (Lee 2010: 313). Even more recently, in 1987, an organization proposed to create the State of Cumberland, which includes several counties in Upper East Tennessee (Claiborne, Hancock, and Hawkins), southwest Virginia (Lee, Scott, and Wise), and southeastern Kentucky (Bell, Harlan, and Knox) (see Figure 20).

We see, thus, how the perception of East Tennessee as a distinct entity has historical roots that have impacted the current 'sense of place' (cf. Gieryn 2000; Agnew 2002). Sectional differences manifest themselves in personal identity, and for East Tennessee, this personal identity difference has echoes of place memory (cf. Lewicka 2008). Most residents of Tennessee believe that the Grand Divisions, and East Tennessee in particular, are separated by profound cultural differences. John Shelton Reed, a noted sociologist of the South, explains that regional identity is the "cognitive entity that people use to orient themselves"

---

[20] See McKinney (1978) for an elaboration of this idea.

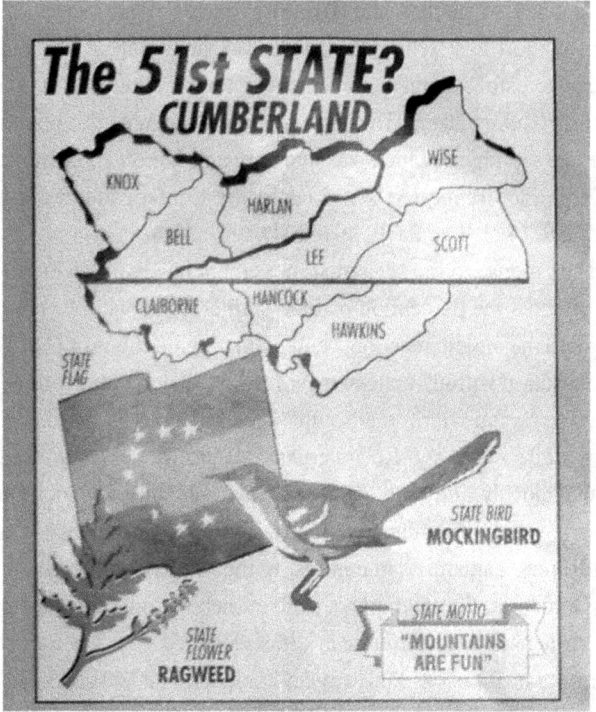

Figure 20 The proposed State of Cumberland.

(Reed 1983: 11). That is, cultural difference – whether based on perception or based on some concrete reality – helps people orient themselves and define themselves as distinct. Ask a Tennessean where he/she is from, and the response will most likely specify at least the Grand Division. For some, it is the particular subregion that is highlighted, for example, 'Upper East Tennessee' or 'North East Tennessee.' There is a palpable sense of difference in the minds of state residents, even if, as Montgomery (1995: 70) notes "though just about everyone native to the state, regardless of social class, *knows* that these divisions are there in very human terms, it is usually right nigh impossible for them to pin down what they consist of" (emphasis in original).

6.4 Linguistic Patterning of Place-Based Features in East Tennessee

In prior publications, place-based identity, rootedness, emerges as a significant predictor of features such as the monophthongization of /aɪ/ (Reed 2020a), both the relative frequency and realization of rising pitch accents (Reed 2020b), and aspects of the Southern Vowel Shift (Reed 2018b). Since the findings demonstrate that place attachment affects the presence and realization of features in the speech of participants, an analysis of how they negotiate the various meanings of *place* in Appalachia, more generally, and East Tennessee and Hancock County, more specifically and how these negotiations create and/or delineate social differentiation is critical to understanding the phonetic variation observed and its broader social implications.

Hancock County participants indeed have a strong sense of localness, and this sense has an observable linguistic impact. However, this community is not monolithic; some participants are quite attached to place while others are less attached to place, so the place has somewhat disparate meanings, depending upon the individual (cf. Gieryn 2000). Thus, to truly understand the complex nature of place attachment – why speakers feel attached to this place – and sense of place – what place means to them – we should consider how the individual participants respond and contextualize *place* in their responses about Hancock County. Responses examined below represent answers to interview questions about participants' feelings toward Hancock County, and their responses illuminate the conflicting view of Appalachia as one's home to cherish or as an object of disparagement (cf. Cramer (2018) and Luhman (1990) for Kentucky). Additionally, participants expressed their awareness that sounding a particular way indexed Hancock County and, as a result, contributed to this contested meaning. Observing individual responses as expressing contested and sometimes contradictory sentiments permits us to frame why linguistic features play a prominent role in the discussion of *place*, especially *place* in East Tennessee, and why rootedness is crucial to some residents in this community.

Full demographic information and rootedness scores by participant are provided in the Online Appendix. The median rootedness score among my participants was 28. Thus, we can use that number as a dividing line in the discussion that follows. Those speakers with scores below 28 will be considered less rooted, and those with scores 28 and above will be considered more rooted. Where applicable and illuminating, I will note the division between these two groups.[21] Often, participants share similar views, but the nuance of the discussion and what they focus on in their responses reveals the complex nature of place orientation in this community. Where relevant in the discussion, the participants' rootedness classification will be placed in parentheses after the name (e.g., Rachel (more rooted)), to facilitate comparison between the more rooted and less rooted speakers.

Many of the participants identify most strongly with communities within their local community of Hancock County, followed closely by East Tennessee or

---

[21] Example recordings of more and less rooted speakers where one can hear the subtle differences (Sounds 17a–d) are available at www.cambridge.org/EISO_Carmichael

Upper/North East Tennessee. These participants consider the local area and East Tennessee as central to their self-perceptions, and notably, they are not as aligned with the rest of Tennessee or the broader South. Numerous participants express how sounding a certain way implies belonging. Some participants express pride in their language, Edward (more rooted) noting "this is how we talk, there's nothing wrong with it," and Tyler (less rooted) said "it's like artwork, man, I love it!." Two responses that directly speak to how language, place, and identity are intertwined stand out – Juanita, a long-time educator states that "you know you're from here when you start talking like us," and Tyler also states, "we have this tone that sounds familiar." And yet, as with many stigmatized and misunderstood varieties, speakers here express a range of opinions regarding the variety. Some folks mention how much the local region and community mean to them, reflecting a place-based identity. Other participants, however, describe efforts to avoid sounding like a "country bumpkin," or "hillbilly," or refer to their own "bad grammar," "country slang," or perhaps "horrible sound." Such varied responses indicate that standard language ideologies (Lippi-Green 2012) have made quite an impact on speakers' perceptions. But, at the same time, pride in the local variety is also present, a theme probed in the analysis that follows.

6.4.1 Conflicting Conceptions of Place

Participant narratives reflected a tension between pride and stigma, following the contradictions of meaning as discussed in work on indexical fields (Eckert 2008) and attitudinal cognitorium (Preston 2010, and see Section 4.2). Many participants expressed pride in being from Hancock County and recognized a distinction from other areas, particularly the more rooted speakers. However, there was an attendant admission from most participants that the county has shortcomings and is far from perfect. Many of the most negative comments came from the less rooted speakers, and often they speak of how hard it might be to overcome the issues. In contrast, the more rooted speakers sound more optimistic, pointing out that they felt that the county could overcome the problems and issues. It is a fine balancing act that many participants do, praising the county and its people while also engaging in critique. Occasionally, a compliment hastily followed a critique to ameliorate what was said. At other times, a critique immediately mitigated a compliment.

Many of the less rooted speakers seem to focus on the stigma and the more negative side. James, a less rooted sixty-nine-year-old, referring to himself, said that Hancock County was "a part of you wherever you go." However, he noted that many people did not feel the same, and he mentioned that he considered leaving the county. He mentioned several times how the size of the county and the lack of opportunity make life more challenging. Also, he mentioned that people seem to look down on Hancock County and its people, primarily due to poverty. Brian, a less-rooted thirty-year-old, acknowledged that where one is born and raised has an indelible impact. This admission is not one of full and unmitigated acceptance. He also acknowledged the dearth of career and recreational opportunities in the county though he realizes that it might be in "bad taste" to tell me that. Brian also shared that while Hancock County and East Tennessee "were home" for him, he was contemplating moving away. He had spent some time away in Middle Tennessee, and he was actively considering relocation. His mother warned him that he would finally realize how distinct the people were in the mountains as compared to elsewhere. She warned him that not everyone in Middle Tennessee would be as friendly and welcoming as "mountain people," particularly those in the large metropolitan area where he was considering. He agreed with this assertion but did not necessarily point out any concrete examples of difference. However, he believed that he might need to leave for better opportunities.

At the other end of the rootedness continuum, Edward, a seventy-year-old more-rooted speaker, called Hancock County the "best place in the world to grow up" and said that he was "proud to have been raised and educated in Hancock County." He discussed the "freedom" that the area and its people enjoyed, particularly during his childhood. Yet, he also points to many problematic issues, such as widespread poverty and drug abuse, but stated that he felt that the county could overcome those issues, particularly if locals could "see what we have here." Similarly, Martha, a seventy-three-year-old more-rooted female, stated that Hancock is "remote and rural" and that "we've been looked down on," yet she loved the county and could not envision living anywhere else. She quite poignantly stated "where you are is part of who you are," and Hancock County was part of her.

In these discussions, we see that both sets of speakers note positives and negatives. However, the less rooted speakers feel that the negatives, and the stigma that comes along, might outweigh the positives. Thus, many mentioned plans to leave (e.g., Brian) or said that they had considered leaving (e.g., James). Contrastingly, more-rooted speakers acknowledged the negatives, but they did not see the unfavorable aspects of Hancock County fatalistically. Rather, they emphasized the favorable aspects and talked about overcoming any detriments.

Many participants, while describing the internal tensions regarding the area, exhibited the influence of circulating negative tropes. By using terms widely associated with derision of the region (e.g., "hillbilly" and being "from the backwoods"), these participants reflected an internalization of widely propagated stereotypes of Appalachia itself. Juanita, a less rooted fifty-year-old, discussed layers of Hancock County and the broader East Tennessee region, noting, "We have such natural and cultural beauty" and yet she acknowledged that "problems still exist." And these problems, primarily stemming from historical and systemic poverty and its ramifications, color perceptions of the area. Alluding to circulating stereotypes, she discussed not wanting to appear like a "dumb hillbilly" because of where she is from. This is a reference to the idea that people from this area, being the mountains of Appalachia, were somehow less intelligent ("dumb") and perhaps culturally backward ("hillbilly").[22] In the same vein, Trish, a sixty-eight-year-old more-rooted speaker, enjoyed "knowing her neighbors" and "the slower pace of life" within the county. This was all part of "the feeling of community" that characterized the county. Yet, she also noted the problems associated with "remoteness," particularly that some people considered "us" to be "country bumpkins." This term, as above, refers to the idea that people from the mountains are different from urban/suburban dwellers ("country") and are not as sophisticated ("bumpkins"). Shortly after using the term "country bumpkin," she said that when traveling, both nearby and further from home, she proudly stated that she was from Hancock County.

Both more-rooted and less-rooted speakers were familiar with circulating tropes and referenced them in their responses. However, perspectives were slightly different. For example, Juanita said that she did not want to appear as a "dumb hillbilly" while Trish said that others might see her as a "country bumpkin." Trish seemed to find humor in this acknowledgement. But Juanita did not want to *personally* appear as a hillbilly. For Trish, others may view her and other Hancock Countians negatively, whereas Juanita seemed to indicate that she herself might appear negative. These two perspectives are related, but the nuance of the point of view demonstrates the difference in the speaker cohort. More-rooted speakers acknowledge the possible stigma from outsiders but do not appear to internalize it, while less rooted speakers often lament that they are part of the stigma.

6.4.2 A Changing Place

In practically every interview, participants noted that Hancock County was changing. Many different reasons and explanations emerged, but three factors seemed to be the central drivers of change: a loss/drift in local civic pride, loss of local neighborhoods, and in-migration. Typically, more rooted participants referenced the changing nature of civic pride. Referring to my (Paul's) peer generation of the late 1990s and early 2000s, Edward (more rooted) lamented that "younger people don't have the same pride as y'all did." He believed the

---

[22] See Montgomery and Heinmiller (2021) for the various meanings and senses of the term 'hillbilly' in Appalachia.

presence of civic pride was something that helped to counteract more negative perceptions of the county and stereotypes about the region. Some of his commentary could be considered typical longing for the good old days, yet he described something more. The local pride had its roots in a feeling of distinctiveness, which he felt helped to combat and possibly alleviate the negative perceptions of the county. He singled out and used as examples the county's successful high school basketball teams, who for a period of years were highly competitive in the state playoffs. He stated, referring to me (Paul) and the teams I played for, "you boys cared about this county, and other people did too." Edward seems to indicate here that the success of the teams buttressed, and was perhaps driven by, local pride. However, the athletic success waned, and apparently, so too did the local pride. Rachel, a more rooted thirty-five-year-old, offered a similar opinion, commenting on the fact that attendance at local sporting events was diminishing. She made the connection between pride and going to local events, and she also noted that the lack of attendance reflected a loss of local pride. She stated, "you go to a game and there's like a couple dozen people there." This was somewhat shocking to me, as previously the games would be very well attended. When asked what happened, she responded, "people just don't seem to care anymore."

Other more rooted participants attributed the change to a loss of localness. One of the prevailing reasons given was school consolidation, by which the county, over the last few decades, consolidated all the local community elementary schools into a single unified elementary school. As recently as the 1960s, the county had over forty elementary schools in various areas of the county. These smaller schools, according to many participants, particularly the more rooted participants, cultivated a strong sense of localness. Misty, a more rooted thirty-seven-year-old female, stated, "We're not tight little communities anymore... We're losing our localness." She specifically referenced the closing of the local schools as one way the county was losing this 'localness.' While she saw the obvious cost benefits of a single school, she felt strongly that a loss of localness, an unintended consequence of school consolidation, was negative. Other participants echoed similar sentiments.

In-migration also featured prominently in all discussions of *place*. 'Outsiders,' that is, folks not from Hancock county moving in – a term used by almost every participant – have had a significant impact on Hancock County, and many participants lamented this. It seemed, from the perspective of some participants, that the traditional families were being displaced. James, a less rooted sixty-nine-year-old, described the feeling, "You look around, and some of the historical last names are just not here anymore." Such a change was not easy, and some participants offered ideas about why the change was difficult. Nathan, a less rooted forty-year-old said "a lot of the beauty and what we love about the place, a lot of people don't want to share that with outsiders." Such a profound statement might be regarded as purely antagonistic toward outsiders. Nathan, however, also mentioned his disapproval of this sentiment. He pointed out how some natives to the county were somewhat "close-minded," and too "set in their ways." He felt that outsiders could have positive impacts, but that depended on the individual.

Relatedly, what most people seemed to resent was the attitude of some outsiders. According to Trish (more rooted), "outsiders want to change things" within the county and "people who move in complain" about the county. Misty (more rooted) also described the presence of in-migrants in the school system, noting that "I don't know any last names anymore." Her main issue with not knowing the students and their parents was that it was hard for her to address parents' complaints by just picking up the phone and calling them. The lack of these relationships complicated many issues at school and elsewhere.

Discussions of in-migration were not always negative. Some told anecdotes about outsiders "fitting in" well if they wanted to. This sentiment was echoed by many, that outsiders could fit in and would be welcomed if they approached the community without condescension. Nonetheless, even those outsiders who fit in symbolized to participants that the county was changing. "The county is not the same as when I grew up" noted James (less rooted). He had many "outsiders" as neighbors that he "got along well" with, yet it "wasn't how it used to be." He did not necessarily see this as negative, however, rather representative of change in progress.

6.4.3 Impact of Standard Language Ideologies and External Stigma

Although the language is a defining characteristic of the county, the impact of standard language ideologies is also very present. Some participants used negative terminology when describing the local speech. Additionally, many shared anecdotes of ridicule for the way they spoke. It is noteworthy that both more and less rooted speakers showed the influence of standard language ideologies in this regard. However, more rooted speakers seemed more resentful of the ridicule, and, consequently, more determined to speak in a local way. Less rooted speakers were also angry, but it seemed that they felt that explanation of the differences or accommodation might be better options. Lippi-Green (2012) describes Southerners (and by extension we might assume Appalachians) participating in derision and stigmatization of local accents, and that some Southerners choose to speak differently. However, the impact of rootedness would seem to complicate this idea, where more rooted speakers appear to reject stigmatization. These speakers do not appear to see any reason to change, and in fact, stigma and ridicule seem to encourage the use of local speech as a reaction against these negative perceptions.

Many participants talked of "bad grammar," "country accent," or as above, "hillbilly language." However, even though many similar terms were used, a difference between more and less rooted speakers remains. Rachel (more rooted) somewhat sheepishly admitted that she initially did not want to be interviewed, as she was afraid that how "bad" she talked would be noticed. She feared being seen as a "country bumpkin" or as "Ellie Mae" from the *Beverly Hillbillies*.[23] After assurances that neither her nor her speech were to be judged, and I (Paul) reemphasized my own localness, she willingly agreed. She said that she was self-conscious of her speech because of her "bad English." However, even though she thought it was "bad," she did not necessarily feel that a change was necessary. Contrast this with Haley (less rooted) who talked about her own "awful speech." She described hearing a recording of herself and wondering, "do I sound that bad?." She felt that others would see her and people who spoke like her as "uneducated hicks." She wondered if changing her speech might help her avoid some stigma.

Other less rooted speakers referred to the local language as incorrect or as lacking something compared to a more educated variety of English. For example, Tyler, a less rooted thirty-five-year-old male talked about "dropping g's," a reference to the alternation between /n/ and /ŋ/. Many talked about not "talking correct" or "not using good English." Joey (less rooted) talked about the difference between "country versus proper," with local speech being country and elsewhere being proper. "Proper" was better, although many local people spoke "country." Such labels reveal, sadly, entrenched standard language ideologies about what language is *supposed* to be (cf. Lippi-Green 2012). The derisive terms used for local language belie a belief by some that local language is aberrant.

In contrast, more rooted speakers did acknowledge (like Rachel above) that local speech may be seen as sounding uneducated or might be considered "bad English," but that did not mean that it was of no value. Edward (more rooted) said that the "slow drawl" of local speech derived from the county's "mountainness." He knew that the way he talked may not seem educated, but he "has never been ashamed" and openly questioned why someone would be. Trish (more

---

[23] This program, which ran from 1962–1971, followed a family from the Ozarks who relocated to Beverly Hills after finding oil on their lands. Many humorous plots revolved around the misunderstandings and miscommunications between the 'hillbillies' and the 'city folk.' A reference to this show demonstrates the power of popular media portrayals of the South, particularly a show based primarily on stereotypes (Lippi-Green 2012).

rooted) acknowledged that education might "make a difference," but she also questioned why someone would feel like they needed to change.

Two powerful stories came when participants related the impact or anticipation of ridicule. The reactions to the ridicule reveal the differences between more rooted and less rooted speakers. One very poignant story came from Haley, a less rooted speaker. She had gone to a nearby college (approximately 50 miles from Hancock County). For one class, she had to record a voice-over for a presentation. She recalled thinking "oh no," and that she was very hesitant about the project. Her fears were realized, as other students began to laugh and giggle as her voice described the animations and presentation slides. One student in particular said out loud "you sound so funny!." Realizing that such a statement might be hurtful, this other student quickly attempted to mitigate her laughter, stating, "I don't mean to offend," yet reiterated that Haley's manner of speaking was humorous. Naturally, such commentary and laughter were incredibly painful. Haley defended her speech and said to me "I'm not embarrassed by it, but I know that it will always be an issue." Such ridicule, and lasting impact from it, occurs repeatedly with respect to Appalachian speakers.[24] Haley felt that she might need to accommodate her speech to "something more standard" to avoid further ridicule.

Misty (more rooted) spoke of her concerns about pursuing a graduate degree. She said, "I was scared about going on for my Master's, because of the way I talk." She was equating sounding local as incommensurate with a graduate school education. She felt that sounding a certain way would hinder her or would somehow block her ability to continue her education. She had concerns about how other students and professors might treat her. She wondered if she would be taken seriously in a graduate program sounding like she was from Hancock County. However, she did say that she decided that ridicule or laughter would not stop her from achieving this personal goal, saying "I'm proud of where I'm from." She did finish her degree, and she said that getting the degree did not change her speech, which she noted was a source of pride. She appreciated sounding like someone from Hancock County.

These anecdotes show that standard language ideologies (Lippi-Green 2012) have had quite the impact. The negative terminology utilized and the plaintive anecdotes of ridicule reflect that some people feel (or are made to feel) that the way they speak is lesser. Yet, the reactions from participants highlight the differences between more and less rooted speakers.

---

[24] See for example, Underhill (1975) for linguistic discrimination in the corporate world, Ayers (1996) for other anecdotes from academia, and Greene (2010), particularly the preface, for similar stories from other mountain speakers.

6.4.4 Pride in Local Speech

Although many participants shared some negative sentiment about the local speech, or worse, had experienced mockery of their own speech, many spoke with great regard for local speech. The regard had several expressions: the belief that local speech preserved an older form of English, the belief that local speech was distinct, and the belief that sounding local was important. For each of these aspects of pride, the reactions and explanations of more and less rooted speakers differed.

A few speakers, mainly less rooted speakers, referenced the antiquity of mountain speech as a source of pride. Brian (less rooted) said that local speech was "the language of old." Juanita (less rooted) spoke of the "Elizabethan" nature of the speech of Hancock County and other mountain areas. She said it was "very much like the KJV."[25] Such a reference most likely refers to antiquity, although perhaps also piety. A few others also referenced some gloried past when describing local speech.

Such arguments are not new – authors have often compared Appalachian English to Elizabethan English, Chaucerian English, or some other variety from the distant past (e.g., Frost 1899; Campbell 1921; Kephart 1922; among others). However, many participants seemed to be using the supposed antiquity or historical nature of speech to fight back against stereotyping. I (Paul) know this argument well, as I have personally used it in the past. If something has roots in a glorious past, it becomes more difficult to ridicule. In fact, less rooted speakers seem to use this strategy to undermine the mockery. Lack of knowledge of the 'historical' nature of the speech is what drives the ridicule. Thus, speakers who are aware of the historical nature of local speech can feel better about themselves and their speech. If the mockers knew that local speech was like that of the great English bard, the ridicule might stop. While such ideas are not accurate, they nonetheless demonstrate that speakers want to have pride in the way they speak. Local speakers search for ways to legitimize their speech in the eyes of others, and history is one way.

Many speakers expressed the belief that Hancock County has a distinct way of speaking. Here, rootedness plays into how speakers view the implications of such distinction. Charlotte (less rooted), who moved to the county as a child, recounted that she felt like Hancock Countians spoke differently, "the language stood out to me when we moved in." Terry (less rooted) described the county as having "our own dialect." He felt this made people stick out, and he was not sure whether this was a good or bad thing. At the other end of the rootedness continuum, Edward (more rooted) said that "language is a part of Hancock"

---

[25] She was referring to the King James Version of the Bible.

and that "we get our slow drawl from our mountain-ness." He was proud of the language, even though he knew that some might view it negatively.

Both more and less rooted speakers noted the distinctive nature of Hancock County speech. Less rooted speakers tended to try to justify the distinctiveness as a type of linguistic preservation. In contrast, more rooted speakers tended to state that the distinctiveness derived from place. Less rooted speakers noted the differences but did not necessarily view the differences positively. However, the more rooted speakers like Edward note the distinctiveness with pride. Speech set Hancock County apart and being set apart was positive.

The perceived distinctiveness was often highlighted when traveling. Martha (more rooted) said that "we don't realize it's different until we go somewhere." Trish (more rooted) said that, when traveling, "people stared because they had never heard anyone talk like that." Many people had stories of being asked where they were from while on vacation after someone heard them speak. Most of these were narrated as humorous anecdotes. Trish and Edward (both more rooted) are married. They separately told me the same story. While traveling out west, they were waiting for a table in a restaurant. They were talking to one another, and a person walked up and said, "you must be from the mountains of Tennessee or Virginia." Somewhat dumbfounded, the couple asked him how he knew. He replied, "I'm from [a nearby town] and you sound just like home." Naturally, they were thrilled to hear that. Importantly, this anecdote points out the emotional connection that speakers have to local speech. To sound like home refers to an emotional link between a particular way of speaking and a (presumably) cherished place. Tyler (less rooted), who had to interview lots of people for his work, talked about how he needed to change for outsiders, "if I am trying to talk, to prove to you and show that I am not a hillbilly, that definitely changes how I talk." He knew that some people might stigmatize him if he did not alter his speech.

Not only was local speech distinctive, many saw language as one of the defining characteristics of the county, if not the defining characteristic. Juanita (less rooted) said that "you know you're from around here when you start talking like us." Referring to in-migration and acceptance, she continued "outsiders belong when they use mountainisms." Tyler (less rooted) said that the local language could be described as a principal aspect of local culture. These descriptions demonstrate that the populace is keenly aware that their speech is central to what it means to belong or to be considered local. I note here that these very insightful comments came from less rooted speakers. Even though their attachment to the local area may not be as strong as other speakers, less rooted speakers were still readily aware of how prominently speech featured into localness. To sound local is to belong, and such belonging is of prime importance to residents.

Sounding local was of paramount importance to many participants. Tyler (less rooted) said that people tend to perceive someone who uses local speech features – "that tone that sounds familiar" – differently. Local speech can put people at ease because it "sounds like home." Part of his work required much interaction and one-on-one interviewing. He overtly referred to speech as the vehicle to demonstrate belonging and localness. He said, "someone considered an outsider or not from the area, you're not gonna get anywhere close to the same interview." Despite his weaker personal tie to the area, he noticed the importance of sounding local.

However, many respondents also noted that not everyone in the community sounded the same, and these responses uncovered further differences between more and less rooted speakers. Many pointed to local speech being more prevalent in older speakers. Trish (more rooted) stated that many older people "had that country accent" and that not all younger people did. She considered this a loss for the younger generation. Contrast this sentiment with that of Brian (less rooted) who stated that "the older generation" sounds a certain way. He seemed to indicate that change was happening among younger speakers, and it was not necessarily negative. Terry (less rooted) talked of "some having it [local speech features] more than others." He thought it might be an urban/rural split. Here, I think he means the town dwellers versus those who live further from town, as there is no real urban area in Hancock County. Terry continued, saying that he had friends who "intentionally change the way they speak" after moving away. He noticed that "they sound odd" to him now, that they do not sound local anymore. He insinuated that this change was negative. He thought they might have sounded different before they moved, but he was unsure. Others, however, referred more to a sense of local attachment with respect to speech. Edward (more rooted) said "those that don't identify [and] don't have the same pride, don't sound the same." Part of being local meant sounding local.

6.5 Conclusions

The discussion above has highlighted differences, in the aggregate, between more and less rooted speakers. Fundamentally, more rooted speakers have an overall more positive view of the county and its speech, showing how *place* as distinctive and something to orient toward is important. This connects with the history, as East Tennessee and the mountain area being distinct from the rest of the state, and perhaps the South, is important and is something to highlight. In contrast, the opinions of less rooted speakers are more mixed. While not always overtly negative, many less rooted speakers acknowledge stigma and negative aspects, and some note the impact of both. Again, these sentiments connect with history, as the roots of stigma and being seen as negatively different have roots in the events of the past. Modern speakers, both more and less rooted, recognize the connection to East Tennessee as being distinct as a place. However, their discursive ways of signaling belonging show the conflicting meanings of *place*.

7 Urban or Rural, Rooted or *Un*rooted, What's Local Is Local: Summarizing Case Study Themes

The two case studies presented above come from quite different locales: one is urban/suburban, the other is rural; one population is mobile and changing, the other is immobile and rooted; one is situated in marshland along the coast, the other represents an inland mountain enclave. We see in both analyses, however, how elements from sociolinguistics and allied fields discussed in this Element have been mobilized in the interest of deepening engagement with language and place, thereby producing a more nuanced understanding of the linguistic situation in both locales.

In both areas, participants actively constructed their sense of place via language practices (and linguistic perceptions). That said, the physical and geographic correlates of *place* were also significant in each locale. In Chalmette, for example, the physical – but also saliently psychosocial – border of water and rivers created the enclave community where nonstandard Yat features were able to persist a generation longer than within city limits. In East Tennessee, there are officially recognized borders – of Appalachia more broadly and of the Grand Division more locally. Yet, the imagined borders of being backwoods have a clear relevance. Upper East Tennessee is not an official designation, but the imagined community (Anderson 2006) is clearly defined and oriented toward. And crucially demonstrated within participants' commentary about language and place, there exists a strong desire to show membership to this imagined community via focusing on the positive aspects of what it means to be *rooted* in the mountains of East Tennessee. What was essential to understanding the attachments to, and orientations toward, these various places, at various scales, was engaging with the ways participants defined themselves and others in relation to these locales. In the case of Greater New Orleans, we could see this via physical maps being drawn – which included and excluded, highlighted and erased, certain parts of the broader community in significant and visibly evident ways. In East Tennessee, the imagined quality of cultural and linguistic distinctiveness has an actual source in geography, and the subjective source in history and culture – you must (literally) cross a mountain to get to the next town. Thus, Hancock County is geographically separate, and by extension, culturally separate and unique.

In both locales, memory and personal connection to *place* are manifestly important. For Greater New Orleans, the background to any discussion about the city is the tragedy of Hurricane Katrina and the ongoing gentrification that has followed this disaster, rendering authentic claims to New Orleans as a place ever more valuable. The nostalgia culture that has arisen after Katrina is central to understanding the key oppositions between newcomers and longstanding residents. In East Tennessee, history and memory are intertwined. The history of this region has led to ideologies of distinctness within the broader landscape of the state – this distinctness, of course, plays out linguistically and otherwise. But part of how this sense of place comes to connect with individuals, and their own personal history, is via their memories of their homeplace, and how rooted they are in that place over generations; that is, rootedness implies a personal connection to a place as well as lineage over time linking one's personhood to that place. Notably, participants' individual rootedness in Hancock County mediates both how they use place-linked linguistic features and how they discuss their homeplace.

A key backdrop to the linguistic ecosystem in Greater New Orleans is the angst surrounding New Orleans becoming less distinctive, less representative of its former sense of place, given the incoming population of "from anywhere" arrivals. As locals battle it out for the right to define what New Orleans is as a place, and who has a claim to it, language becomes a key tool in the artillery. And indeed, this idea is not specific to this locale. Because language practices develop in-place, and come to be signifiers of speakers' *emplacèdness*, they also become part of the sense of place – the soundscape of that place – and speakers are able to agentively mobilize these resources as a symbolic expression of their authentic claim to that place. As researchers more broadly examining post-disaster, in-migration contexts make sense of the changes they observe in these situations, we suggest that language is a key indicator of identity and allegiance, and an agentive component of the continued processes of placemaking.

In the Hancock County case study, the subjectivity of *place* – particularly through place memory – was central to understanding rootedness. The meanings of place were different for different people – home, East Tennessee, or something else – and tended to relate to particular experiences and remembrances of the county. That is, central to the *current* conceptions of Hancock County's sense of place are the memories of that place, handed down via the stories told within the community. These differing ideas of Hancock County's identity as a place, for some residents, dovetails with opposition (us/them;

newcomer/longtimer, etc.) in the discussions of in-migration and out-migration. Many of the speakers openly mentioned the tension between the newer arrivals and longstanding residents – which points directly to who has 'rightful' access to defining the identity of a place. Furthermore, there was the rather clear distinction for some speakers of 'us' and 'them' in opposition, particularly with respect to future directions of the county. Central to these discussions of both leaving and staying were ideas about the functionality or utility of Hancock County as a place, particularly with respect to recreation and economic opportunity. Often, this discussion also included aspects of aesthetics. The natural beauty of the mountains was framed as a benefit; however, residents also discussed the fact that mountains create difficulties with respect to travel and business access. And, as some local residents leave the county and more newcomers arrive, we also see a clear worry about a changing place, echoing the concerns over placelessness seen elsewhere. Long-standing residents of the county are concerned with losing those things that they feel make the county special, and thus becoming less distinct. Others view change as inevitable, and express a belief that perhaps being more like other places could be beneficial.

In both locales, the linguistic patterns observed contribute to a shared – and continuously evolving – sense of place. We assert that by considering individuals' relationships with the locales being studied, we gained insights into the linguistic variation within each community while also capturing something very real about the way they experience the world. Perspectives on *place* can be central to identity construction, and can set up the forms of opposition, categorization, and cognitive frameworks through which individuals orient themselves to both the physical landscape and the community members who populate that space. By engaging with the varied ways that humans process *place* – the cognitive structures we use, as we log sensory experiences and memories in our minds; the emotions we tie to aesthetic aspects of our surroundings; the connections we build between the physical landscape and its inhabitants; and the (dis)comfort we may experience upon registering different subjective views on a given place that we view as belonging to us, and us to it – we add depth and nuance to our sociolinguistic analyses.

8 Conclusions and Future Directions

In this Element, we have strived to provide a thorough – even if by definition incomplete – description of how *place* has been conceived of in sociolinguistic research up to now, with the goal of drawing attention toward similar conversations that appear to be happening in varied pockets of the field of sociolinguistics, without the necessary awareness of a coherent subfield of interest: the sociolinguistics of place. We have further tried to contextualize such research by documenting *place* as an object of study across disciplines – sociology, geography, political science, anthropology, landscape architecture, and beyond – noting that *place* is considered and conceptualized differently within and across these fields. While this diversity of approaches can provide an invigoratingly interdisciplinary 'conceptual melting pot' of tools for thinking about *place*, it can also present challenges via differing terminologies and priorities across fields (cf. Patterson & Williams 2005). Above, we have tried to identify some of the core ideas that have been influential across fields, and to note the ways that researchers in the sociolinguistics of place might mobilize these conceptualizations in our own work. Via two case studies, we have illustrated how place theory has informed linguistic analyses in our respective fieldsites: Post-Katrina Greater New Orleans and Hancock County in East Tennessee, arguing that without the lens of place theory, the linguistic patterns in both locales cannot be adequately understood. We assert that *place* – whether mobilized via place identity, place attachment, place orientation, sense of place, or place-making – is a significant element in all sociolinguistic research, and advocate for its further theorization by sociolinguists.

8.1 Finding a Place for 'Place' in (Socio)linguistic Research

While completing the literature review for this Element, two notable conclusions became apparent to us: (1) The study of *place* is inherently interdisciplinary and belongs to no single field; this is because place is implicit in everything that can be studied, and different fields at different points in time chose to render place *explicit* in their examinations in different ways. Thus, to capture the varied approaches to *place*, and the ways in which it has been theorized, one must by definition read widely in geography, architecture, anthropology, sociology, environmental psychology, and so on. (2) The study of *language and place*, within the subfield of sociolinguistics, feels similarly disjointed, despite in theory representing a singular disciplinary lens on *place*. It happened more than once that we found two studies very much in conversation with each other, with similar goals, sometimes even arriving upon similar conclusions at the same time, without recognizing that the other existed. This is, in part, our goal for writing this Element – to bring together these varied voices on language and place, and informing them that indeed, they are part of this conversation; by recognizing that, we can propel the field forward in terms of the ways we theorize the role of *place* in sociolinguistics. We encourage researchers to acknowledge that connection via their chosen keywords, whether that be 'sense of place,' 'language and place,' 'place attachment,' 'place orientation,' 'place identity,' 'place-making,' 'sociolinguistics of place' or even just *'place'* – thereby signaling participation in a broader conversation about language and place.

We also urge *place* researchers in sociolinguistics to create more clear 'homes' for our work – the establishment of the *Journal of Linguistic Geography* in 2013 suggests a watershed moment in the identification of this subfield and its significance to linguistics (and its recent establishment as open access invites more engagement with other fields). We propose an accompanying annual or biennial conference to bring researchers on language and place together to foster further conversations and connections to continue advancing the field. Many of the edited volumes on language and place derive from organized sessions at conferences or special themed editions of existing conferences (e.g., Montgomery & Moore 2017; Cornips & de Rooij 2018), but to make the kind of gains that would generate broader awareness and relevance of linguistic perspectives on *place* to those outside of our field, **we need a place for discussions about language and place**.

8.2 Finding a Place for Linguistics in the Study of Place

Although this Element is geared toward sociolinguists who wish to deepen their engagement with place theory, we also hope to encourage all linguists to consider the ways we can look outward, to other fields, offering linguistic tools to the study of place. Perhaps understandably, a significant proportion of work on *place* in fields like geography and architecture centers on the physicality of the place, its aesthetic qualities, and/or the experience of moving through that space. However, Tuan (1991) crucially issued a call to human geographers to consider the role of language in the social construction of *place*; a call that has mostly gone ignored. Tuan calls this a narrative-descriptive approach, but we would argue that what he was actually calling for was a linguistic approach. Tuan (1991: 684) writes:

> Overwhelmingly the discipline [of human geography] has emphasized the economic and material forces at work. Neglected is the explicit recognition of the crucial role of language, even though without speech humans cannot even begin to formulate ideas, discuss them, and translate them into action that culminates in a built place.

We draw our readers' attention to this gap in the field in order to build momentum behind what we see as a driving question moving forward: "what can linguistics offer to researchers interested in *place*?" As the field of linguistics as a whole remains small and relatively siloed within the humanities and social sciences, we suggest sharing the tools of linguistic analysis with *place* researchers in other fields, as a means of rendering our work in linguistics more broadly accessible and legible to other social scientists. This, in turn, benefits the discipline, especially in light of the looming threats against the humanities in higher education, securing our relevance to those who simply do not understand or value linguistic examination for its own sake. Moreover, we would argue that language is indeed just as central to place-making as some of the other measures being used across fields examining place right now. That is to say, we genuinely believe that linguistics has something to offer these other fields, in that language is central to *place*; thus, their theories of *place*, lacking a linguistic component, are incomplete at present. It is our hope that linguists can bridge this gap to improve our understanding of the relationship between two key defining aspects of the human experience: language and place.

References

Agha, Asif. 2003. The social life of cultural value. *Language and Communication* 23: 231–273.

Agnew, John. 1987. *Place and Politics: The Geographical Mediation of State and Society*. Routledge.

Agnew, John. 2002. *Place and Politics in Modern Italy*. The University of Chicago Press.

Anderson, Benedict. 2006. *Imagined Communities: Reflections on the Origin and Spread of Nationalism*. Verso.

Appadurai, Arjun. 1990. Disjuncture and difference in the global economy. *Theory, Culture, & Society* 7(2–3): 295–310.

Appalachian Regional Commission (ARC). 2023. www.arc.gov. Last accessed October 27, 2023.

Arefi, Mahyar. 1999. Non-place and placelessness as narratives of loss: Rethinking the notion of place. *Journal of Urban Design* 4(2): 179–193.

Arefi, Mahyar. 2013. The structure of visual difference: A comparative case study of Mariemont and Lebanon, Ohio. *Urban Design International* 18(4): 296–312.

Auer, Peter. 2010. Language and space: The neogrammarian tradition. In Peter Auer & Jurgen Erich Schmidt (eds.), *Language and Space: An International Handbook of Linguistic Variation, Vol. 1: Theories and Methods*, Mouton de Gruyter. 70–87.

Auer, Peter. 2013. The Geography of Language: Steps toward a New Approach. *FRAGL* 2013. www.sdd.uni-freiburg.de/fragl/2013.16/.

Ayers, Edward L. 1996. What we talk about when we talk about the South. In Edward L. Ayers, Patricia Nelson Limerick, Stephan Nissenbaum, & Peter S. Onuf (eds.), *All over the Map: Rethinking American Regions*, John Hopkins University Press. 62–82.

Bailey, Guy, Tom Wikle, Jan Tillery, & Lori Sand. 1996. The linguistic consequences of catastrophic events: An example from the Southwest. In Jennifer Arnold, Renée Blake, Brad Davidson, Scott Schwenter, & Julie Solomon (eds.), *Sociolinguistic Variation: Data, Theory, and Analysis*, CSLI. 435–451.

Bakhtin, Mikhail. 1981. *The Dialogic Imagination: Four Essays*. Michael Holquist, ed. University of Texas Press.

Baranowski, Maciej. 2023. Part of town as an independent factor: The NORTH-FORCE merger in Manchester. *Language Variation & Change* 34(3): 239–269.

Barnes, Sonia. 2016. Negotiating local identity: Rural migration and sociolinguistic perception in urban Asturias. *Lengua y migraci* 8(2): 45–77.

Basso, Keith H. 1996a. *Wisdom Sits in Places: Landscape and Language among the Western Apache.* University of New Mexico Press.

Basso, Keith H. 1996b. Wisdom sits in places: Notes on a Western Apache landscape. In Steven Feld & Keith H. Basso (eds.), *Senses of Place*, School of American Research Press. 53–90.

Beaman, Karen. 2021. Identity and mobility in linguistic change across the lifespan: The case of Swabian German. In Arne Ziegler, Stefanie Edler, Nina Kleczkowski, & Georg Oberdorfer (eds.), *Urban Matters: Current Approaches of International Sociolinguistic Research (Studies in Language Variation)*, John Benjamins. 27–60.

Becker, Kara. 2009. /r/ and the construction of place identity on New York City's Lower East Side. *Journal of Sociolinguistics* 13(5): 634–658.

Becker, Kara. 2014. The social motivations of reversal: Raised BOUGHT in New York City English. *Language in Society* 43(4): 395–420.

Becker, Kara & Luiza Newlin-Lukowicz. 2018. The Myth of the New York City Borough Accent: Evidence from Perception. *University of Pennsylvania Working Papers in Linguistics* (Selected papers from NWAV 46) 24(2): Article 3.

Benheim, Jaime & Annette D'Onofrio. 2024. Local features, local meanings: Language ideologies and place-linked vocalic variation among Jewish Chicagoans. *Language in Society* 53(1): 129–155.

Benor, Sarah. 2010. Ethnolinguistic repertoire: Shifting the analytic focus on language and identity. *Journal of Sociolinguistics* 14(2): 159–183.

Benson, Erica. 2003. Folk linguistic perceptions and the mapping of dialect boundaries. *American Speech* 78: 307–330.

Bergeron, Paul H., Stephen V. Ash, & Jeanette Keith. 1999. *Tennesseans and Their History.* University of Tennessee Press.

van Bezooijen, Renée & Charlotte Gooskens. 1999. Identification of language varieties: The contribution of different linguistic levels. *Journal of Language and Social Psychology* 18: 31–48.

Blommaert, Jan. 2016. From mobility to complexity in sociolinguistic theory and method. In Nikolas Coupland (ed.), *Sociolinguistics: Theoretical Debates*, Cambridge University Press. 242–259.

Blommaert, Jan & Ben Rampton. 2011. Language and superdiversity. *Diversities* 13(2): 1–23.

Blu, Karen I. 1996. "Where do you stay at?": Home place and community among the Lumbee. In Steven Feld & Keith H. Basso (eds.), *Senses of Place*, School of American Research Press. 197–227.

Bortoni-Ricardo, S. M. 1985. *The Urbanization of Rural Dialect Speakers. A Sociolinguistic Study in Brazil.* Cambridge University Press.

Brasseaux, Carl A. 2005. *French, Cajun, Creole, Houma: A Primer on Francophone Louisiana.* Louisiana University Press.

Braithwaite, Ben & Kristian Ali. 2024. The colonial geography of linguistics: A view from the Caribbean. In Anne Charity Hudley, Christine Mallinson, & Mary Bucholtz (eds.), *Decolonizing Linguistics*, Oxford University Press. 62–79.

Britain, David. 2016. Sedentarism, Nomadism and the sociolinguistics of dialect. In Nikolas Coupland (ed.), *Sociolinguistics: Theoretical Debates*, Cambridge University Press. 217–241.

Britain, David. 2017. Which way to look? Perspectives on "urban" and "rural" in Dialectology. In Chris Montgomery & Emma Moore (eds.), *Language and a Sense of Place: Studies in Language and Region*, Cambridge University Press. 171–187.

Brown, Douglas & Barbara Perkins. 1992. Disruptions in place attachment. In Irwin Altman & Setha M. Low (eds.), *Place Attachment*, Plenum Press. 279–304.

Bruggeman, Walter. 2002. *The Land: Place as Gift, Promise, and Challenge in Biblical Faith.* Fortress Press.

Bucholtz, Mary. 2003. Sociolinguistic nostalgia and the authentication of identity. *Journal of Sociolinguistics* 7(3): 398–416.

Bucholtz, Mary & Kira Hall. 2005. Identity and interaction: A sociocultural linguistic approach. *Discourse Studies* 7(4–5): 584–614.

Bucholtz, Mary, Nancy Bermudez, Victor Fung, Lisa Edwards, & Rosalva Vargas. 2007. Hella nor Cal or totally so Cal?: The perceptual dialectology of California. *Journal of English Linguistics* 35(4): 325–352.

Callesano, Salvatore. 2020. *Perceptual Dialectology, Mediatization, and Idioms: Exploring Communities in Miami.* PhD dissertation, University of Texas.

Campanella, Richard. 2006. *Geographies of New Orleans: Urban Fabrics before the Storm.* Center for Louisiana Studies (University of Louisiana at Lafayette).

Campanella, Richard. 2010. *Delta Urbanism: New Orleans.* American Planning Association, Planners Press.

Campbell, John C. 1921. *The Southern Highlander and His Homeland.* The Russell Sage Foundation.

Campbell-Kibler, Kathryn. 2009. The nature of sociolinguistic perception. *Language Variation and Change* 21: 135–156.

Carmichael, Katie. 2014. *"I Never Thought I Had an Accent until the Hurricane": Sociolinguistic Variation in Post-Katrina Greater New Orleans.* PhD dissertation, Ohio State University.

Carmichael, Katie. 2017. Displacement and local linguistic practices: R-lessness in post-Katrina Greater New Orleans. *Journal of Sociolinguistics* 21(5): 696–719.

Carmichael, Katie. 2018. "Since when does the Midwest have an accent?": The role of regional accent and reported speaker origin in speaker evaluations. *English World-Wide* 39(2): 127–156.

Carmichael, Katie. 2020. (æ)fter the storm: An examination of the short-a system in Greater New Orleans. *Language Variation and Change* 32(1): 107–131.

Carmichael, Katie. 2023. Locating place in variationist sociolinguistics: Making the case for ethnographically informed multidimensional place orientation metrics. *Journal of Linguistic Geography* 11(2): 65–77.

Carmichael, Katie & Nathalie Dajko. 2016. Ain't dere no more: New Orleans language and local nostalgia in Vic & Nat'ly Comics. *Journal of Linguistic Anthropology* 26(3): 1–24.

Carter, Erica, James Donald, & Judith Squires. 1993. *Space and Place: Theories of Identity and Location.* Lawrence & Wishart.

Carter, Phillip M., Lydda López Valdez, & Nandi Sims. 2020. New dialect formation through language contact: Vocalic and prosodic developments in Miami English. *American Speech* 95(2): 119–148.

Carver, Craig M. 1987. *American Regional Dialects: A Word Study.* University of Michigan Press.

Cassidy, Fred & Joan Houston Hall. 1985–2013. *Dictionary of Regional American English* (DARE), Volumes I–VI. Belknap Press of Harvard University Press.

Castle, Emery, Junjie Wu, & Bruce Weber. 2011. Place orientation and rural–urban interdependence. *Applied Economic Perspectives and Policy* 33(2): 179–204.

Cedergren, Henrietta. 1973. *The Interplay of Social and Linguistic Factors in Panama.* PhD dissertation, Cornell University.

Chambers, J. K. 2000. Region and language variation. *English World-Wide* 21(2): 169–199.

Chang, Ailsa, Christopher Intagliata, & Sarah Handel. 2022. New Zealand considers changing its name to confront its troubled colonial past. *National Public Radio.* www.npr.org/2022/08/05/1115627020/new-zealand-maori-aotearoa-colonization-name-change-petition.

Charity Hudley, Anne, Christine Mallinson, & Mary Bucholtz (eds.). 2024. *Decolonizing Linguistics.* Oxford.

Clapson, Mark. 2013. *The Plan for Milton Keynes.* Routledge.

Clopper, Cynthia & David B. Pisoni. 2004. Homebodies and army brats: Some effects of early linguistic experience and residential history on dialect categorization. *Language Variation & Change* 16(1): 31–48.

Clopper, Cynthia & David B. Pisoni. 2006. Effects of region of origin and geographic mobility on perceptual dialect categorization. *Language Variation & Change* 18(2): 193–221.

Clopper, Cynthia & David B. Pisoni. 2007. Free classification of regional dialects of American English. *Journal of Phonetics* 35(3): 421–438.

Coles, Felice Anne. 2001. The authenticity of Yat: A "real" New Orleans dialect. *Southern Journal of Linguistics* 25: 74–86.

Cornips, Leonie & Vincent de Rooij (eds.). 2018. *The Sociolinguistics of Place and Belonging: Perspectives from the Margins*. John Benjamins.

Cotter, William & Uri Horesh. 2015. Social integration and dialect divergence in coastal Palestine. *Journal of Sociolinguistics* 19(4): 460–483.

Coupland, Nikolas (ed.). 2010. *The Handbook of Language and Globalization*. Wiley-Blackwell.

Cramer, Jennifer. 2016. *Contested Southernness: The Linguistic Production and Perception of Identities in the Borderlands*. Publication of the American Dialect Society 100. Duke University Press.

Cramer, Jennifer. 2018. Perceptions of appalachian English in Kentucky. *Journal of Appalachian Studies* 24(1): 45–71.

Cramer, Jennifer. 2021. Mental maps and perceptual dialectology. *Language & Linguistics Compass* 15(2): 1–15.

Cramer, Jennifer & Chris Montgomery (eds.). 2016. *Cityscapes and Perceptual Dialectology: Global Perspectives on Non-linguists' Knowledge of the Dialect Landscape*. Mouton de Gruyter.

Crawford, Charles W. 1986. The nature of the Volunteer state: What makes Tennessee different? *The Egyptians 1985–1986 Yearbook*. 61–70.

Cresswell, Tim. 2015. *Place: An Introduction* (2nd ed.). Wiley Blackwell.

Dajko, Nathalie & Katie Carmichael. 2023. Plus ça change ... Perceptions of New Orleans English before and after the storm. *Journal of English Linguistics* 51(2): 95–132.

De Caro, Frank. 1992. New Orleans, Folk ideas, and the lore of place. *Louisiana Folklore Miscellany*, Volume VII: 68–80.

Diener, Alexander & Joshua Hagen. 2021. The power of place in place attachment. *Geographical Review* 112(1): 1–5.

Dillard, J. L. 1985. Language and linguistic research in Louisiana. In Nicholas Spitzer (ed.), *Louisiana Folklife: A Guide to the State*, Moran Colographics. 41–42.

Dong, Jie & Jan Blommaert. 2009. Space, scale and accents: Constructing migrant identity in Beijing. *Multilingua* 28: 1–24.

D'Onofrio, Annette. 2015. Persona-based information shapes linguistic perception: Valley Girls and California vowels. *Journal of Sociolinguistics* 19(2): 241–256.

D'Onofrio, Annette & Jaime Benheim. 2019. Contextualizing reversal: Local dynamics of the Northern Cities Shift in a Chicago community. *Journal of Sociolinguistics* 24(4): 469–491.

Drager, Katie & James Grama. 2014. "De tawk dakain ova dea": Mapping language ideologies on O'ahu. *Dialectogia* 12: 23–51.

Duchêne, Alexandra & Monica Heller. 2012. *Language in Late Capitalism: Pride and Profit*. Routledge.

Duncan, Daniel. 2019. The influence of suburban development and metropolitan fragmentation on language variation and change: Evidence from Greater St. Louis. *Journal of Linguistic Geography* 7: 82–97.

Eble, Connie. 2006. Speaking the Big Easy. In Walt Wolfram & Ben Ward (eds.), *American Voices: How Dialects Differ from Coast to Coast*, Blackwell. 42–48.

Eckert, Penelope. 1989. *Jocks and Burnouts: Social Categories and Identity in the High School*. Teachers College Press.

Eckert, Penelope. 2004. Variation and a sense of place. In Carmen Fought (ed.), *Sociolinguistic Variation: Critical Reflections*, Oxford University Press. 107–118.

Eckert, Penelope. 2008. Variation and the indexical field. *Journal of Sociolinguistics* 12(4): 453–476.

Eckert, Penelope. 2012. Three waves of variation study: The emergence of meaning in the study of sociolinguistic variation. *Annual Review of Anthropology* 41: 87–100.

Eckert, Penelope & Sally McConnell-Ginet. 1992. Think practically and look locally: Language and gender as community-based practice. *Annual Review of Anthropology* 21: 461–490.

Eeckhout, Bart. 2001. The "Disneyification" of Times Square: Back to the future? In Kevin Fox Gotham (ed.), *Critical Perspectives on Urban Redevelopment*, Elsevier Press. 379–428.

Evans, Betsy. 2004. The role of social networks in the acquisition of local dialect norms by Appalachian migrants in Ypsilanti, Michigan. *Language Variation and Change* 16: 153–167.

Evans, Betsy. 2013. Seattle to Spokane: Mapping perceptions of English in WA. *Journal of English Linguistics* 41(3): 268–291.

Evans, Betsy. 2016. City talk and country talk: Perceptions of urban and rural English in Washington state. In Jennifer Cramer & Chris Montgomery (eds.), *Cityscapes and Perceptual Dialectology: Global Perspectives on Non-linguists' Knowledge of the Dialect Landscape*, Mouton de Gruyter. 55–72.

Evans, Betsy, Erica Benson, & James Stanford (eds.). 2018. *Language Regard: Methods, Variation and Change*. Cambridge University Press.

Farrington, Charlie. 2019. *Language Variation and the Great Migration: Regionality and African American Language*. PhD dissertation, University of Oregon.

FOX8 Staff. 2023. Chalmette local infuses Waze navigation with homegrown humor and charm. https://www.fox8live.com/2023/08/06/chalmette-local-infuses-waze-navigation-with-homegrown-humor-charm/ (Last accessed October 23, 2024).

Fried, Marc. 1963. Grieving for a lost home. In Leonard Duhl (ed.), *The Urban Condition: People and Policy in the Metropolis*, Basic Books. 151–171.

Frost, William Goodell. 1899. *Our Contemporary Ancestors in the Southern Mountains*. Atlantic Monthly.

Gieryn, Thomas F. 2000. A place for space in sociology. *Annual Review of Sociology* 26: 463–495.

Gotham, Kevin Fox. 2007. *Authentic New Orleans: Tourism, Culture, and Race in the Big Easy*. New York University Press.

Greene, Rebecca. 2010. *Language, Ideology, and Identity in Rural Eastern Kentucky*. PhD dissertation, Stanford University.

Grenoble, Lenore. 2011. On thin ice: Language, culture and environment in the Arctic. *Language Documentation and Description* 9: 13–34.

Grieser, Jessica. 2022. *The Black Side of the River: Race, Language, and Belonging in Washington, DC*. Georgetown University Press.

Grootaers, Willem. 1959. Origin and nature of the subjective boundaries of dialects. *Orbis* 8: 355–384.

Hall-Lew, Lauren, Amie Fairs, & Alan Lew. 2015. Tourists' attitudes towards linguistic variation in Scotland. In Eivind Torgersen, Stian Hårstad, Brit Mæhlum, & Unn Røyneland (eds.), *Language Variation – European Perspectives V* (Studies in Language Variation (SILV); Vol. 17), John Benjamins. 99–110.

Hay, Jennifer, Aaron Nolan, & Katie Drager. 2006. From fush to feesh: Exemplar priming in speech perception. *The Linguistic Review* 23(3): 351–379.

Hay, Jennifer & Katie Drager. 2010. Stuffed toys and speech perception. *Linguistics* 48(4): 865–892.

Hazen, Kirk. 2002. Identity and language variation in a rural community. *Language* 78(2): 240–257.

Hazen, Kirk. 2020. *Appalachian Englishes in the 21st Century*. West Virginia University Press.

Heller, Monica. 2003. Globalization, the new economy, and the commodification of language and identity. *Journal of Sociolinguistics* 7: 473–492.

Heller, Monica. 2010. The commodification of language. *Annual Review of Anthropology* 39: 101–114.

Hickey, Raymond (ed.). 2020. *The Handbook of Language Contact*, 2nd Ed. Wiley-Blackwell.

Horesh, Uri & Roey Gafter. 2022. Enregisterment of local features in Palestinian Arabic political discourse. Talk given at *Sociolinguistics Symposium 24*. July 13–16. University of Ghent, Belgium.

Hotzenköcherle, Rudolph, Rudolf Trüb, Doris Handschuh, et al. (ed.). 1969–1997. *Sprachatlas der deutschen Schweiz*. Francke-Verlag Bern.

Hua, Zhu. 2017. New orientations to identities in mobility. In Suresh Canagarajah (ed.), *The Routledge Handbook of Migration and Language*, Routledge. 117–132.

Hult, Francis M. & Helen Kelly-Holmes. 2019. Spectacular language and creative marketing in a Singapore tailor shop. *International Journal of Multilingualism* 16(1): 79–93.

Ilbury, Christian. 2021. A tale of two cities: The discursive construction of "place" in gentrifying East London. *Language in Society* 51(3): 1–24.

Inscoe, John C. 2008. *Race, War, and Remembrance in the Appalachian South*. University of Kentucky Press.

Irvine, Judith T. & Susan Gal. 2000. Language ideology and linguistic differentiation. In Paul Kroskrity (ed.), *Regimes of Language: Ideologies, Politics, and Identities*, School of American Research. 35–83.

Jaffe, Alexandra. 2019. Poeticizing the economy: The Corsican language in a nexus of pride and profit. *Multilingua* 38(1): 9–27.

Jeon, Lisa & Patricia Cukor-Avila. 2016. Urbanicity and language variation and change: Mapping dialect perceptions in and of Seoul. In Jennifer Cramer & Chris Montgomery (eds.), *Cityscapes and Perceptual Dialectology: Global Perspectives on Non-linguists' Knowledge of the Dialect Landscape*, Mouton de Gruyter. 97–116.

Jeszenszky, Péter, Carina Steiner, & Adrian Leemann. 2024. Effects of mobility on dialect change: Introducing the Linguistic Mobility Index. *PLOS ONE* 19(4): e0300735.

Johnstone, Barbara. 2004. Place, globalization, and linguistic variation. In Carmen Fought (ed.), *Sociolinguistic Variation: Critical Reflections*, Oxford University Press. 65–83.

Johnstone, Barbara. 2009. Pittsburghese shirts: Commodification and the enregisterment of an urban dialect. *American Speech* 84(2): 157–175.

Johnstone, Barbara. 2010a. Language & geographical space. In Peter Auer & Jurgen Erich Schmidt (eds.), *Language and Space: An International*

Handbook of Linguistic Variation, Vol. 1: Theories and Methods, Mouton de Gruyter. 1–18.

Johnstone, Barbara. 2010b. Indexing the local. In Nikolas Coupland (ed.), *The Handbook of Language and Globalization*, Wiley-Blackwell. 386–405.

Johnstone, Barbara, Jennifer Andrus, & Andrew E. Danielson. 2006. Mobility, indexicality, and the enregisterment of "Pittsburghese." *Journal of English Linguistics* 34(2): 77–104.

Johnstone, Barbara & Scott F. Kiesling. 2008. Indexicality and experience: Variation and identity in Pittsburgh. *Journal of Sociolinguistics* 12: 5–33.

Jones, Loyal. 1994. *Appalachian Values*. Jesse Stuart Foundation.

Jones, Jamila. 2003. *African Americans in Lansing and the Northern Cities Vowel Shift: Language Contact and Accommodation*. PhD dissertation, Michigan State University.

Jones, Benjamin G. 2015. *Perceptual dialectology of New England: Views from Maine and the web*. Unpublished Master's Thesis, University of Kentucky.

Kallen, Jeffrey L. 2011. Changing landscapes: Language, space and policy in the Dublin linguistic landscape. In Adam Jaworski & Crispin Thurlow (eds.), *Semiotic Landscapes*, Continuum International Publishing Group. 41–58.

Kelley, Lucas P. 2012. A divided state in a divided nation: An exploration of East Tennessee's support of the Union in the secession crisis of 1860–1861. *The Journal of East Tennessee History* 84: 3–22.

Kephart, Horace. 1922. *Our Southern Highlanders*. Outing.

Kerswill, Paul. 1993. Rural dialect speakers in an urban speech community: The role of dialect contact in defining a sociolinguistic concept. *International Journal of Applied Linguistics* 3(1): 33–56.

Kerswill, Paul. 2006. Migration and language. In Klaus Mattheier, Ulrich Ammon, & Peter Trudgill (eds.), *Sociolinguistics/Soziolinguistik. An International Handbook of the Science of Language and Society* (2nd Ed.), Vol 3. De Gruyter. 2271–2285.

Kerswill, Paul & Ann Williams. 2000. Creating a new town koine: Children and language change in Milton Keynes. *Language in Society* 29: 65–115.

King, Sharese. 2021. Rethinking race and place: The role of persona in sound change reversal. *Journal of Sociolinguistics* 25(2): 159–178.

Kolker, Andy & Louie Alvarez. 1985. *Yeah, You Rite!* (film). Center for New American Media.

Kunstler, James Howard. 1993. *The Geography of Nowhere: The Rise and Decline of America's Man-Made Landscape*. Simon & Schuster.

Kurath, Hans. 1939. *Handbook of the Linguistic Geography of New England*. Brown University Press.

Labov, William. 1963. The social motivation of a sound change. *Word* 19: 273–309.
Labov, William. 1966. *The social stratification of English in New York City*. Washington DC: Center for Applied Linguistics.
Labov, William. 1972. *Sociolinguistic Patterns*. University of Pennsylvania Press.
Labov, William. 2007. Transmission and diffusion. *Language* 83(2): 344–387.
Labov, William, Sharon Ash, & Charles Boberg. 2006. *The Atlas of North American English: Phonetics, Phonology and Sound Change*. Mouton de Gruyter.
Ladegaard, Hans J. 1998. National stereotypes and language attitudes: The perception of British, American and Australian language and culture in Denmark. *Language and Communication* 18: 251–274.
Landry, Rodrigue & Richard Y. Bourhis. 1997. Linguistic landscape and ethnolinguistic vitality: An empirical study. *Journal of Language and Social Psychology* 16: 23–49.
Lasley, Carrie Beth. 2012. *Catastrophes and the Role of Social Networks in Recovery: A Case Study of St. Bernard Parish, LA, Residents After Hurricane Katrina*. PhD dissertation, University of New Orleans.
Lee, Tom. 2010. The lost cause that wasn't: East Tennessee and the myth of unionist Appalachia. In Andres L. Slap (ed.), *Reconstructing Appalachia: The Civil War's Aftermath*, University of Kentucky Press. Chap. 11, 293–322.
Leeman, Jennifer & Gabriella Modan. 2010. Selling the city: Language, ethnicity and commodified space. In Elana Shohamy, Eliezer Ben-Rafael, & Monica Barni (eds.), *Linguistic Landscape in the City*, Multilingual Matters. 182–198.
Lesho, Marivic & Eeva Sippola. 2018. Toponyms in Manila and Cavite, Philippines. In Thomas Stolz & Ingo Warnke (eds.), *Vergleichende Kolonialtoponomastik: Strukturen und Funktionen kolonialer Ortsbenennung*. Mouton de Gruyter. 317–332.
Lewicka, Maria. 2008. Place attachment, place identity, and place memory: Restoring the forgotten city past. *Journal of Environmental Psychology* 28: 209–231.
Lippi-Green, Rosina. 2012. *English with an Accent: Language, Ideology, and Discrimination in the United States* (2nd Ed.). Routledge.
Lonergan, John. 2016. Real and perceived variation in Dublin English. In Jennifer Cramer & Chris Montgomery (eds.), *Cityscapes and Perceptual Dialectology: Global Perspectives on Non-linguists' Knowledge of the Dialect Landscape*, Mouton de Gruyter. 233–256.

Lou, Jackie Jia. 2016. *The Linguistic Landscape of Chinatown: A Sociolinguistic Ethnography.* Multilingual Matters.

Low, Setha & Irwin Altman. 2012. *Place Attachment.* Palgrave.

Luhman, Reid. 1990. Appalachian English stereotypes: Language attitudes in Kentucky. *Language in Society* 19(3): 331–348.

MacCash, Doug. 2023. Meet the yat behind the "Chalmette HeyBrah" driving app voice. *Times Piccayune*/NOLA.com www.nola.com/entertainment_life/arts/meet-the-man-behind-the-chalmette-heybrah-driving-app-voice/article_3924e834-3187-11ee-b9e8-ab34f5cd6329.html (Last accessed August 10, 2023).

Mallinson, Christine & Becky Childs. 2007. Communities of practice in sociolinguistic description: Analyzing language and identity practices among black women in Appalachia. *Gender & Language* 1(2): 173–206.

Massey, Doreen. 1994. *Space, Place, and Gender.* University of Minnesota Press.

McAndrew, Francis T. 1998. The measurement of "rootedness" and the prediction of attachment to home-towns in college students. *Journal of Environmental Psychology* 18: 409–417.

McClay, Wilfred & Ted V. McAllister. 2014. *Why Place Matters: Geography, Identity, and Civic Life in Modern America.* New Atlantis.

McKeever, Amy. 2020. The heart-breaking, controversial history of Mount Rushmore. *National Geographic.* www.nationalgeographic.com/travel/article/the-strange-and-controversial-history-of-mount-rushmore.

McKinney, Gordon B. 1978. *Southern Mountain Republicans 1865–1900.* University of North Carolina Press.

MacKenzie, Lauren, George Bailey, & Danielle Turton. 2022. Towards an updated dialect atlas of British English. *Journal of Linguistic Geography* 10(1): 46–66.

Mesthrie, Rajend. 1993. Koineization in the Bhojpuri–Hindi diaspora, with special reference to South Africa. *International Journal of the Sociology of Language* 99: 25–44.

Meyerhoff Miriam. 2006. *Introducing Sociolinguistics.* Routledge.

Miller, DeMond Shondell & Jason David Rivera. 2010. Landscapes of disaster and place orientation in the aftermath of Hurricane Katrina. In David L. Brunsma, David Overfelt, & J. Steven Picou (eds.), *The Sociology of Katrina: Perspectives on a Modern Catastrophe*, Rowman & Littlefield. 141–154.

Milroy, James & Lesley Milroy. 1978. Belfast: Change and variation in an urban vernacular. In Peter Trudgill (ed.), *Sociolinguistic patterns in British English*, E. Arnold. 19–36.

Miner Murray, Meghan. 2019. Why Are Native Hawaiians Protesting against a Telescope? *New York Times* www.nytimes.com/2019/07/22/us/hawaii-telescope-protest.html (Last Accessed August 21, 2023).

Modan, Gabriella Gahlia. 2007. *Turf Wars: Discourse, Diversity, and the Politics of Place*. Blackwell.

Monka, Malene, Pia Quist, & Astrid Ravn Skovse. 2020. Place attachment and linguistic variation: A quantitative analysis of language and local attachment in a rural village and an urban social housing area. *Language in Society* 49(2): 173–205.

Montgomery, Michael. 1995. Does Tennessee have three "Grand Dialects"? Evidence from the Linguistic Atlas of the Gulf States. *Tennessee Folklore Society Bulletin* 57: 69–84.

Montgomery, Chris. 2017. Maps and mapping in (perceptual) dialect geography. In Chris Montgomery & Emma Moore (eds.), *Language and a Sense of Place: Studies in Language and Region*, Cambridge University Press. 147–170.

Montgomery, Chris & Emma Moore (eds.). 2017. *Language and a Sense of Place: Studies in Language and Region*. Cambridge University Press.

Montgomery, Michael & Jennifer Heinmiller. 2021. *The Dictionary of Southern Appalachian English*. University of North Carolina Press.

Montgomery, Chris & Phillip Stoeckle. 2013. Geographic information systems and perceptual dialectology: A method for processing draw-a-map data. *Journal of Linguistic Geography* 1: 52–85.

Moriarty, Máiréad. 2014. Contesting language ideologies in the linguistic landscape of an Irish tourist town. *International Journal of Bilingualism* 18(5): 464–477.

Mucciaccio, Francesca. 2009. *"A gaggle a' Y'ats" and other stories: Tracing the effects of ideology on language change through indexical formation in Y'at*. Unpublished Honors Thesis, Reed College.

Mufwene, Salikoko. 2001. *The Ecology of Language Evolution*. Cambridge University Press.

Niedzielski, Nancy. 1999. The effect of social information on the perception of sociolinguistic variables. *Journal of Language and Social Psychology* 18(1): 62–85.

Norberg-Schulz. 1980. *Genius Loci: Towards a Phenomenology of Architecture*. Rizzoli.

Nycz, Jennifer. 2015. Second dialect acquisition: A sociophonetic perspective. *Language and Linguistics Compass* 9(11): 469–482.

Nycz, Jennifer. 2018. Stylistic variation among mobile speakers: Using old and new regional variables to construct complex place identity. *Language Variation and Change* 30: 175–202.

Nycz, Jennifer. 2019. Linguistic and social factors favoring acquisition of contrast in a new dialect. *Proceedings of the 19th International Congress of Phonetic Sciences*, Melbourne, August 2019. 1480–1484.

Orton, Harold. 1960–1980. *The Linguistic Atlas of England*. University of Leeds.

Pabst, Katharina. 2022. *Putting the "Other Maine" on the Map: Language Variation, Local Affiliation, and Co-occurrence in Aroostook County English*. PhD dissertation, University of Toronto.

Park, Sung-Yul Park & Lionel Wee. 2017. Nation-state, transnationalism, and language. In Suresh Canagarajah (ed.), *The Routledge Handbook of Migration and Language*, Routledge. 47–62.

Patterson, Michael & Daniel R. Williams. 2005. Maintaining research traditions on place: Diversity of thought and scientific progress. *Journal of Environmental Psychology* 25(4): 361–380.

Pederson, Lee, Susan L. McDaniel, & Carol M. Adams (eds.) 1986–93. *Linguistic Atlas of the Gulf States*, 7 vols. University of Georgia Press.

Pennycook, Alistair. 2007. Language, localization, and the real: Hip-hop and the global spread of authenticity. *Journal of Language, Identity & Education* 6(2): 101–115.

Pharao, Nicolai, Marie Maegaard, Janus Spindler Møller, & Tore Kristiansen. 2014. Indexical meanings of [S+] among Copenhagen youth: Social perception of a phonetic variant in different prosodic contexts. *Language in Society* 43(1): 1–31.

Pienimäki, Hanna-Mari, Tuomas Väisänen, & Tuomo Hiippala. 2024. Making sense of linguistic diversity in Helsinki, Finland: The timespace of affects in the linguistic landscape. *Journal of Sociolinguistics* 28(2): 3–21.

Plichta, Bartek, & Preston, Dennis R. 2005. The /ay/s have it: The perception of /ay/ as a North-South stereotype in United States English. *Acta Linguistica Hafniensia* 37(1): 107–130.

Podesva, Robert J. 2007. Phonation type as a stylistic variable: The use of falsetto in constructing a persona. *Journal of Sociolinguistics* 11(4): 478–504.

Podesva, Rob. 2011. The California Vowel Shift and gay identity. *American Speech* 86(1): 32–51.

Podesva, Rob & Janneke Van Hofwegen. 2014. How conservatism and normative gender constrain variation in inland California: The case of /s/. *University of Pennsylvania Working Papers in Linguistics* 20(2): 129–137.

Polinsky, Maria. 2018. *Heritage Languages and Their Speakers*. Cambridge.

Preston, Dennis R. 1989. *Perceptual Dialectology: Nonlinguists' Views of Areal Linguistics*. De Gruyter Mouton.

Preston, Dennis R. (ed.). 1999. *Handbook of Perceptual Dialectology: Volume 1*. John Benjamins.

Preston, Dennis R. 2010. Language, people, salience, place: Perceptual dialectology and language regard. *Dialectologia* 5: 87–101.

Proshansky, Harold, Abbe Fabian, & Robert Kaminoff. 1983. Place-identity: Physical world socialization of the self. *Journal of Environmental Psychology* 3: 57–83.

Rapoport, Amos. 1977. *Human Aspects of Urban Form: Towards a Man-Environment Approach to Urban Form and Design*. Oxford.

Reed, John Shelton. 1983. *Southerners: The Social Psychology of Sectionalism*. University of North Carolina Press.

Reed, Paul E. 2016. *Sounding Appalachian: /ay/ monophthongization, Rising Pitch Accents, and Rootedness*. PhD dissertation, University of South Carolina.

Reed, Paul E. 2018a. The importance of Appalachian identity: A case study in rootedness. *American Speech* 93(3–4): 409–424.

Reed, Paul E. 2018b. Rootedness and the Southern Vowel Shift in Appalachia. Paper presented at the American Dialect Society (ADS) Annual Meeting. Salt Lake City, UT. January 4–7.

Reed, Paul. 2020a. The importance of rootedness in the study of Appalachian English: Case study evidence for a proposed rootedness metric. *American Speech* 95(2): 203–226.

Reed, Paul E. 2020b. Inter- and intra-regional variation in intonation: An analysis of rising pitch accents and rootedness. *Journal of the Acoustical Society of America* 147(1): 616–626.

Reed, Paul E. 2020c. Prosodic variation and rootedness in Appalachian English. *University of Pennsylvania Working Papers in Linguistics* 25(2).

Regan, Brendan. 2022. *Guadaloop* or *Guadalupe*?: Place-name variation and place identity in Austin, Texas. *American Speech* 97(4): 441–482.

Relph, Edward. 1976. *Place and Placelessness*. Pion.

Remlinger, Kathryn. 2018. Yooperisms in tourism: Commodified enregistered features in Michigan's Upper Peninsula's linguistic landscape. In Leonie Cornips & Vincent de Rooij (eds.), *The Sociolinguistics of Place and Belonging: Perspectives from the Margins*, John Benjamins. 261–286.

Rensink, Wim G. 1955. Informant classification of dialects. Reprinted in Dennis R. Preston (ed.), *Handbook of Perceptual Dialectology, Vol.1*, John Benjamins. 3–7.

Rickford, John R. & Faye McNair-Knox. 1994. Addressee-and topic-influenced style shift: A quantitative sociolinguistic study. In Douglas Biber & Edward Finegan (eds.), *Sociolinguistic Perspectives on Register*, Oxford University Press. 235–276.

Robley, Christye. 1994. What is Available on Yat: research of local libraries and archives of New Orleans. In Linda DePascual, Jean Greenfield, Susan Miller, et al. (eds.), *New Orleans Neighborhood Talk: Examining the Original Dialects of the New Orleans Ninth Ward Neighborhood*, Loyola University of New Orleans. 33–41.

Ryan, Ellen Bouchard. 1979. Why do low-prestige language varieties persist? In Howard Giles & Robert St. Clair (eds.), *Language and Social Psychology*, Basil Blackwell. 145–157.

Schieffelin, Bambi B. 2018. Language socialization and making sense of place. In Leonie Cornips & Vincent de Rooij (eds.), *The Sociolinguistics of Place and Belonging: Perspectives from the Margins*, John Benjamins. 27–54.

Schilling, Natalie. 2017. Smith Island English: Past, present, and future – and what does it tell us about the regional, temporal, and social patterning of language variation and change? *American Speech* 92(2): 176–203.

Schoux Casey, Christina. 2013. *Postvocalic /r/ in New Orleans: Language, Place, and Commodification*. PhD Dissertation, University of Pittsburgh.

Schoux Casey, Christina. 2016. Ya heard me? Rhoticity in post-Katrina New Orleans English. *American Speech* 91: 166–199.

Schoux Casey, Christina. 2020. De-colonizing New Orleans: Social aid & pleasure club second lines. In Jørgen Riber Christensen, Brian Russel Graham, & Gunhild Agger (eds.), *Life after Lines: Tim Ingold across the Humanities*, Aalborg Universitetsforlag. 99–122.

Schreier, Daniel. 2010. Tristan da Cunha English. In Daniel Schreier, Edgar W. Schneider, Jeffrey P. Williams, & Peter Trudgill (eds.), *The Lesser-Known Varieties of English: An Introduction*, Cambridge University Press. 245–260.

Seale, Elizabeth & Christine Mallinson. 2018. *Rural Voices: Language, Identity, and Social Change Across Place*. Lexington Books.

Shulman, Ari N. 2014. GPS and the End of the Road. In Wilfred McClay & Ted V. McAllister (eds.), *Why Place Matters: Geography, Identity, and Civic Life in Modern America*, New Atlantis. 10–47.

Silverstein, Michael. 2003. Indexical order and the dialectics of sociolinguistic life. *Language & Communication* 23: 93–229.

Silverstein, Michael. 2014. The race from place: Dialect eradication and the linguistic "authenticity" of terroir. In Véronique Lacoste, Jakob Leimgruber, & Thiemo Breyer (eds.), *Indexing Authenticity: Sociolinguistic Perspectives*, Walter de Gruyter. 159–187.

Simons, Robert A., Gary DeWine, & Larry Ledebur. 2017. *Retired, Rehabbed, Reborn: The Adaptive Reuse of America's Derelict Religious Buildings and Schools*. Kent University Press.

Sneller, Betsy. 2019. Where our Fathers are From: Place and Conflict in Sociolinguistic Borrowing. *University of Pennsylvania Working Papers in Linguistics* 25(2).

Solomon, Julie. 1999. *Phonological and Syntactic Variation in the Spanish of Valladolid, Yucatán*. PhD dissertation, Stanford University.

Souther, J. Mark. 2007. The Disneyfication of New Orleans: The French Quarter as facade in a divided city. *The Journal of American History* 94: 804–811.

Stanford, James. 2006. When Your Mother Tongue is Not Your Mother's Tongue: Linguistic Reflexes of Sui Exogamy. *University of Pennsylvania Working Papers in Linguistics* 12.2 (Selected papers from NWAV-34).

Stanford, James. 2009. 'Eating the Food of Our Place': Sociolinguistic loyalties in multidialectal Sui villages. *Language in Society* 38(3): 287–309.

State of Tennessee. 2015. Tennessee State Code – annotated. via *LexisNexis*.

Steiner, Carina, Péter Jeszenszky, Viviane Stebler, & Adrian Leemann. 2023. Extraverted innovators and conscientious laggards? Investigating effects of personality traits on language change. *Language Variation & Change* 35(1): 1–28.

Stilgenbauer, Judith. 2015. Processscapes: Dynamic placemaking. In Jeff Hou, Ben Spencer, Thaisa Way, & Ken Yocom (eds.), *Now Urbanism: The Future City Is Here*, Routledge. 92–106.

Tang, Hoa K. 2020. Linguistic landscaping in Singapore: Multilingualism or the dominance of English and its dual identity in the local linguistic ecology? *International Journal of Multilingualism* 17(2): 152–173.

Tennessee Blue Book. 2013. *Tennessee Blue Book 2013–14*. Secretary of State of Tennessee.

Tillery, Jan, Guy Bailey, & Tom Wikle. 2004. Demographic change and American dialectology in the twenty-first century. *American Speech* 79(3): 227–249.

Toth, Gary. 2014. Place conscious transportation policy. In Wilfred McClay & Ted V. McAllister (eds.), *Why Place Matters: Geography, Identity, and Civic Life in Modern America*, New Atlantis. 48–58.

Trudgill, Peter. 1974. *The Social Differentiation of English in Norwich*. Cambridge University Press.

Trudgill, Peter. 1986. *Dialects in Contact*. Oxford: Blackwell.

Trudgill, Peter. 2020. Sociolinguistic typology and the speed of linguistic change. *Journal of Historical Sociolinguistics* 6(2): 1–13.

Trudgill, Peter, Elizabeth Gordon, Gillian Lewis, & Margaret Maclagan. 2000. Determinism in new-dialect formation and the genesis of New Zealand English. *Journal of Linguistics* 36: 299–318.

Tseng, Amelia & Lars Hinrichs. 2021. Introduction: Mobility, polylingualism, and change: Toward an updated sociolinguistics of diaspora. *Journal of Sociolinguistics* 25(5): 649–661.

Tuan, Yi-Fu. 1977. *Space and Place: The Perspective of Experience*. University of Minnesota Press.

Tuan, Yi-Fu. 1980. Rootedness versus sense of place. *Landscape* 24(1):3–8.

Tuan, Yi-Fu. 1991. Language and the making of place: A narrative-descriptive approach. *Annals of the Association of American Geographers* 81(4): 684–696.

Ujang, Norsidah. 2012. Place attachment and continuity of urban place identity. *Procedia – Social and Behavioral Sciences* 49: 156–167.

Underhill, David. 1975. Yukking it up at CBS. *Southern Exposure* 2: 68–71.

US Department of the Interior. 2015. *Secretary Jewell Announces Nation's Highest Peak Will Now Officially Bear Native Name.* www.doi.gov/pressreleases/secretary-jewell-announces-nation%e2%80%99s-highest-peak-will-now-bear-native (Last accessed August 21, 2023).

Villarreal, Dan. 2016 "Do I sound like a valley girl to you?" Perceptual dialectology and language attitudes in California. In Valerie Fridland, Tyler Kendall, Betsy Evans, & Alicia Beckford Wassink (eds.), *Speech in the Western States: Volume 1 The Coastal States*, Publication of the American Dialect Society (PADS) 101: 55–75.

Villena-Ponsoda, Juan-Andrès & Matilde Vida-Castro. 2020. Variation, identity and indexicality in southern Spanish: On the emergence of a new variety in urban Andalusia. In Massimo Cerruti & Stavroula Tsiplakou (eds.), *Intermediate Language Varieties: Koinai and Regional Standards in Europe*, John Benjamins. 149–182.

Wade, Lacey, David Embick, & Meredith Tamminga. 2023. Dialect experience modulates cue reliance in sociolinguistic convergence. *Glossa Psycholinguistics* 2(1): 1–30.

Wagner, Heinrich. 1958–1969. *The Linguistic Atlas and Survey of Irish Dialects*. 4 Vols. Dublin Institute for Advanced Studies.

Walker, Frank X. 2000. *Affrilachia*. Old Cove Press.

Walker, Robyn C. 2007. An alternative construction of identity: A study of place-based identity and its implications. *American Communication Journal* 9(3): 1–17.

Wang, Suosheng, Shengrong Chen, & Honggang Xu. 2019. Resident attitudes towards dark tourism, a perspective of place-based identity motives. *Current Issues in Tourism* 22(13): 1601–1616.

Warren, Paul. 2016. *Uptalk: The Phenomenon of Rising Intonation*. Cambridge University Press.

Wolfram, Walt. 1969. *A Sociolinguistic Description of Detroit Negro Speech*. Center for Applied Linguistics.

Wolfram, Walt. 1997. *Hoi Toide on the Sound Soide: The Story of the Ocracoke Brogue*. University of North Carolina Press.

Works Projects Administration (WPA). 1939. *Tennessee: A Guide to the State*. Viking Press.

Yang, William & R. E. Asher. 1995. Chinese linguistic tradition. In E. Koerner & R. E. Asher (eds.), *Concise History of the Language Sciences: From the Sumerians to the Cognitivists*, Elsevier. 41–45.

Zhang, Qing. 2008. Rhotacization and the "Beijing Smooth Operator": The social meaning of a linguistic variable. *Journal of Sociolinguistics* 12: 201–222.

Acknowledgments

Katie: I am grateful, first and foremost, to the residents of Greater New Orleans who provided data and insights towards the development of my case study. My research was made possible by a National Science Foundation Grant (BCS-1749217) and several seed grants from Virginia Tech. I also thank Virginia Tech, and in particular VT's TOME program, for providing open-access funding for this volume. I thank my parents, Dennis Carmichael and Rosey Buckley Carmichael, for providing essential childcare while I collected data, and I thank my husband Jack Rosenberger for letting me whisk our kids away to New Orleans regularly for fieldwork trips (also thank you Jack for generating the maps in my case study!). I am grateful to Nathalie Dajko and Shawanda Williams, as well as the broader 504 Voices team, for their help in sorting through insights about New Orleans language and culture. Thanks also to the LCUGA 2019 organizers who invited Paul Reed and me to present on language and place, where we were able to expand and refine the thoughts that led to this volume. I thank the Elements editors Rajend Mesthrie and Valerie Fridland, as well as two anonymous reviewers, for their helpful feedback as we formulated our thoughts. And lastly, I thank my collaborator Paul Reed for always being down to 'talk place' with me, and being a neverendingly encouraging and gracious coauthor throughout the writing process.

Paul: I am exceedingly grateful to many, and I must start with residents of the homeland – Hancock County, TN in Appalachia. Your voices and words are the heart of my work, and I am humbled to be able to share them with the world. I give immense thanks to my wife, Dr. Kristin Reed, whose unwavering support and encouragement were and are integral to everything I do. Like Katie, I thank the LCUGA 2019 organizers for inviting us to be plenary speakers, discussing place and language and workshopping our case studies, and conversations there led to this volume. Both editors, Rajend Mesthrie and Valerie Fridland, have been great to work with, and I thank them heartily, and I appreciate the comments from the two anonymous reviewers. And I am grateful to work with Katie Carmichael, whose insights are sharp, whose wit is sharper, whose encouragement and inspiration never falter, and who routinely helps me understand place in a better way.

Cambridge Elements

Sociolinguistics

Rajend Mesthrie
University of Cape Town

Rajend Mesthrie is Emeritus Professor and past head of Linguistics and Research Chair in Linguistics at the University of Cape Town. He was President of the Linguistics Society of Southern Africa (2002–2009) and of the International Congress of Linguists (2013–2018). Among his publications are *The Cambridge Handbook of Sociolinguistics World Englishes* (with R. Bhatt). He was co-editor of *English Today* and editor of the Key Topics in Sociolinguistics series.

Valerie Fridland
University of Nevada, Reno

Valerie Fridland is a Professor of Linguistics at the University of Nevada, Reno. She is the author of *Like, Literally, Dude: Arguing for the Good in Bad English,* and co-author of *Sociophonetics* and lead editor of *Speech in the Western States* series. Her blog, Language in the Wild, appears with *Psychology Today* and her lecture series, Language and Society, is available through The Great Courses.

About the Series

Sociolinguistics is a vital and rapidly growing subfield of Linguistics that draws on linguistics, sociology, social psychology, anthropology and cultural studies. The topics covered in *Cambridge Elements in Sociolinguistics* showcase how language is shaped by societal interactions and in turn how language is a central part of social processes.

Cambridge Elements

Sociolinguistics

Elements in the Series

Conversations with Strangers
William Labov with Gillian Sankoff

Dialectology and the Linguistic Atlas Project
Allison Burkette

Language and Place
Katie Carmichael and Paul E. Reed

A full series listing is available at: www.cambridge.org/EISO